Basic
Adult
Survival
English

with orientation to american life

PART TWO

ROBERT E. WALSH

Prentice-Hall, Inc., Englewood Cliffs, New Jersey 07632

Library of Congress Cataloging in Publication Data

Walsh, Robert E. (date)
  Basic adult survival English.

  1. English language—Text-books for foreign speakers.
2. Americanisms.   I. Title.   II. Title: American life.
PE1128.W34   1984   428.2′4   83–19046
ISBN 0–13–056812–0 (v. 1)
ISBN 0–13–056854–6 (v. 2)

Editorial/production supervision and
   interior design: Elizabeth H. Athorn
Cover design: Ben Santora
Manufacturing buyer: Harry P. Baisley
Interior art: Virgilio Salvador and Don Martinetti
Page layout: Charles Pelletrau

Printed in the United States of America

10   9   8   7   6   5   4   3   2   1

ISBN 0-13-056854-6

Prentice-Hall International, Inc., *London*
Prentice-Hall of Australia Pty. Limited, *Sydney*
Editora Prentice-Hall do Brasil, Ltda., *Rio de Janeiro*
Prentice-Hall Canada Inc., *Toronto*
Prentice-Hall of India Private Limited, *New Delhi*
Prentice-Hall of Japan, Inc., *Tokyo*
Prentice-Hall of Southeast Asia Pte. Ltd., *Singapore*
Whitehall Books Limited, *Wellington, New Zealand*

Contents

3. WORK:

4. DRIVING:

5. COMMUNITY SERVICES:

Preface

Basic Adult Survival English (BASE) is a high-beginning to intermediate level survival ESL textbook in two volumes. It is designed to provide adult learners with basic language proficiency, survival skills, and information about life in the United States. It is particularly aimed at helping newcomers to the United States to become functioning members of American society.

BASE can serve as a core text, providing a foundation for the study of basic ESL, or it may be used as a convenient and effective supplement to existing texts. BASE may be used "cover to cover": Chapters develop in complexity of content and grammar, with continual built-in review of preceding material. It is also possible to pull out individual chapters, such as the Health Care chapter from *Part One* or the Driving chapter from *Part Two*, and use them independently.

The two volumes of BASE are each divided into five chapters that deal with essential survival areas. Each chapter topic is treated thoroughly, with continuity from first page to last. Key features of BASE are as follows:

- Situational conversations present natural language in relevant settings.
- New vocabulary is presented primarily through pictures.
- Structure sections present grammar points and provide practice through examples, writing exercises, and paired student activities.
- Orientation sections explain aspects of American life and offer ideas on coping with a new social and cultural environment. The language used reinforces content and structures presented in the particular chapter. Topics include, for example, "The American Family" and "Taking Care of Your House" in *Part One* or "Buying on Credit" and "Finding a Job" in *Part Two*. Orientation sections may also be used for reading practice.
- Action Sequences engage the student in the ordered physical performance of activities, such as "Taking the Bus" and "Spraying for Insects" in *Part One* or "Buying Coffee from a Vending Machine" in *Part Two*.
- Self-Tests enable students to evaluate their progress as they proceed through the text.

• Listening and Speaking pages at the end of each chapter offer students practice in discriminating and producing English sounds occurring in the chapter.

Each chapter is prefaced by a statement of its curriculum objectives: competencies, orientation topics, and structures. Teacher notes at the beginning of each chapter offer suggestions for use and additional classroom activities.

Introductory Notes and Suggestions for Teachers

Teacher Notes and Suggestions sections at the beginning of each chapter of BASE give page-by-page recommendations of approaches and particular points of emphasis. Here are some general suggestions for use of the text.

1. Before referring to any printed page, the class should first practice orally the language involved. The teacher may want to present and practice beforehand structures and vocabulary to be introduced, or may want to have them learned in context. When a page is set in a particular context, that context should be explained to the students to aid in the transition from oral to written language.

2. Conversations or dialogues may be effectively presented as described below. After setting the situation of the dialogue, and perhaps explaining new vocabulary, the teacher introduces the dialogue orally following these steps:

   • Teacher models dialogue, students listen.
   • Teacher models dialogue, students repeat.
   • Class performs dialogue, half of class taking one side, half the other, repeating after the teacher.
   • Class performs dialogue again on teacher's visual cue.
   • Teacher takes one side of dialogue, class other.
   • Student-student pairs model dialogue for class.
   • Class divides into pairs and practices dialogue; teacher listens.

   The written dialogue may be referred to for reinforcement at any point that the teacher sees it is necessary.

3. Vocabulary on vocabulary pages should be presented with realia when possible. Words may be practiced using a great variety of techniques, including visuals, picture cards, dyads, memory games, association exercises, and so on.

4. Orientation Notes: The teacher first sets the context, relating the topic to the particular lesson. The teacher introduces the point in his/her own words and whenever possible relates the topic to the students' experience and native customs. The teacher then reads the passage in sections and explains it, asking comprehension questions. Then the teacher reads the page line by line and has the students repeat. The teacher should foster class discussion. Passages may later be used for reading practice.

5. Action Sequences: An effective procedure for presenting and practicing Action Sequences is as follows:

   • Teacher says and acts out each step; students watch and listen. (The teacher may wish to pantomime the entire sequence first.)
   • Teacher says and acts out each step; class repeats.
   • Teacher acts out each line and class says each line.
   • Individual students perform the sequence in front of the class saying each line.
   • Individual students perform the sequence in front of the class as seated students in turn give them commands.

   The printed page should be referred to at the appropriate point for reinforcement.

6. Self-Tests can be administered as the teacher desires. Dictations and other tests can be made up by drawing from the text.

7. Listening and Speaking exercises at the end of each chapter cover all the common consonant sounds in initial and final positions and all the common vowel sounds and diphthongs. All words on any one page are drawn from the chapter involved. Additional sound contrasts can be practiced by referring to Listening and Speaking pages previously studied. Pronunciation difficulties will vary for students of different language groups; the teacher should give problem sounds special emphasis. Words in Part C have been syllabicated on the basis of pronunciation.

THE ENGLISH ALPHABET

a b c d e f g h i j k l m n o p q r s t u v w x y z

A B C D E F G H I J K L M N O P Q R S T U V W X Y Z

a b c d e f g h i j k l m n o p q r s t u v w x y z

A B C D E F G H I J K L M N O P Q R S T U V W X Y Z

NUMBERS

1	one	11	eleven	30	thirty	1st	first
2	two	12	twelve	40	forty	2nd	second
3	three	13	thirteen	50	fifty	3rd	third
4	four	14	fourteen	60	sixty	4th	fourth
5	five	15	fifteen	70	seventy	5th	fifth
6	six	16	sixteen	80	eighty	6th	sixth
7	seven	17	seventeen	90	ninety	7th	seventh
8	eight	18	eighteen	100	one hundred	8th	eighth
9	nine	19	nineteen	200	two hundred	9th	ninth
10	ten	20	twenty	1,000	one thousand	10th	tenth
		21	twenty-one	10,000	ten thousand		
		22	twenty-two	100,000	one hundred thousand		
				1,000,000	one million		

DAYS
Monday
Tuesday
Wednesday
Thursday
Friday
Saturday
Sunday

MONTHS
January
February
March
April
May
June

July
August
September
October
November
December

Telephones and Emergencies

chapter one

COMPETENCIES:
1. Answer the telephone and make calls
2. Make long-distance calls
3. Call for assistance in emergency situations and give necessary information
4. Give physical description of people

ORIENTATION:
1. Telephones and telephone service
2. Manner of speaking on telephone
3. Recourses available in emergency situations

STRUCTURES:
1. Placement of adjectives
2. Indefinite articles

Teacher Notes and Suggestions

Pages 3 to 4   Preface by discussing telephones. Ask students how many had telephones in their country or know how to use a telephone. Explain that in America it's necessary for everyone to use telephones. These pages give example conversations for three possibilities: the person called answers the phone (example 1); the person called is home but another person answers (example 2); the person called is not home (example 3). (Other possibilities are wrong number and busy signal.) Present and practice the conversations orally first, acting them out for the class.

Page 4 to 5   In the Orientation Notes, first ask how many students had telephones in their country, whether it was hard to get telephone service, and what the procedure was. Discuss. Then ask how many students have telephones now and how they got them. Read and discuss the first section. Then read and discuss long distance calling. You may want to go into more detail on calling procedures, times, and rates.

Pages 6 to 7   Explain what to do in emergency situations. Give students telephone numbers for their city. Make sure that every student can give the requested information with clear pronunciation. Some work with cross streets may be necessary.

Pages 8 to 12   Set the context, then act out the situations.

Page 14   Use the situation as a means of presenting and practicing vocabulary.

Page 15   If possible, use realia to present clothing vocabulary. See suggestions page *viii*.

Page 16   Use actual colors in teaching color words. Practice with colors of students' clothing. Point out the position of the adjective before the noun modified. Also explain use of the article.

Page 17   1. Explain the situations—giving a description of someone who has committed a crime—then practice the conversations.
2. Activity: Arrange for a student to run in from outside the classroom, grab a purse from someone, and run out. Then ask the class, "What happened?" and "What did he look like?" and see how well they observed and can describe the thief.

Talking on the Telephone

Practice these conversations.

Sorry, wrong number.

1. "This is _____."

3. "He's not here."

a.

Hello.

Hello. May I speak to Tom?

He's not here.

When will he be back?

In about two hours.

Thank you. I'll call back later.

b.

Hello.

Hello. Is Tom there?

No, he's not. Who's calling?

This is Bill. Please tell him to call me.

OK. What's your number?

727–5548

Orientation Notes: *TELEPHONES*

Read and discuss.

Almost every American house and office has a telephone. People can talk to their friends or take care of business on the telephone. It's very convenient.

Telephone service

It's easy to get telephone service for your house or apartment. When you're going to move into a new place, go to the telephone company office and tell them you want to get a telephone. They will ask you a lot of questions. You have to tell them what kind of telephone you want (*dial* or *pushbutton,* table phone or wall phone) and what kind of service you want (usually *regular* service). They will give you a telephone to put in your house, or they will send someone to your house to *install* (put in) a phone.

Paying for service

You usually have to pay a deposit when you start telephone service. The company will send you a bill every month. Telephone service is not expensive, but if you make a lot of long distance calls it can be very expensive.

Long distance

A long distance call is a telephone call to a place far away. You can call long distance from your home phone. First dial the *area code* for the city you're calling, then dial the telephone number. If you call long distance on weekends or late at night it's cheaper. Don't forget about *time zones*. The United States is a big country and the time is different in different parts of the country.

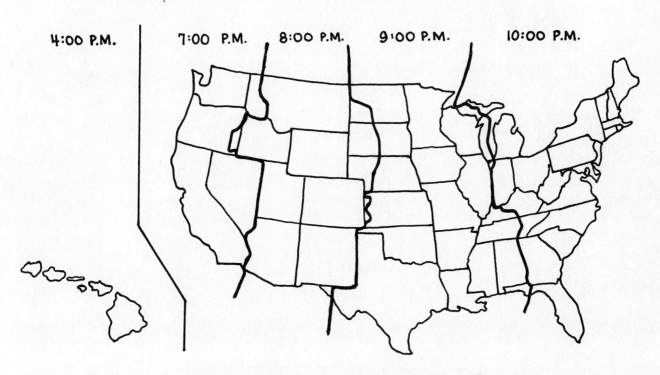

If you don't have money to pay for a long distance call, you can call *collect* and the other person can pay. Talk to the operator first.

Answer these questions and discuss them.

1. Did you have a telephone in your country?
2. What kind of telephone do you have?
3. Do you make a lot of long distance calls? Who do you call? Where?
4. When is the cheap time to call long distance?

Emergency

Read and discuss.

In an emergency you can call:

POLICE _____

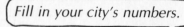
Fill in your city's numbers.

FIRE _____

AMBULANCE _____
(PARAMEDICS)

Or you can call:

OPERATOR _____

They will ask you:

What's your name?
Where do you live?
What's your address?
What's the cross street?

Study this example.

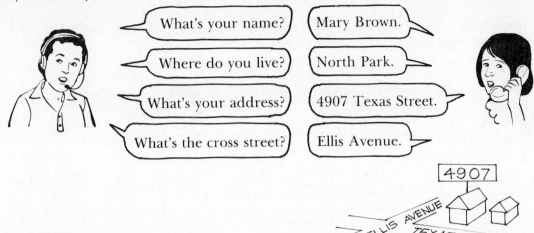

What's your name?	Mary Brown.
Where do you live?	North Park.
What's your address?	4907 Texas Street.
What's the cross street?	Ellis Avenue.

Now answer for yourself, then practice with another student.

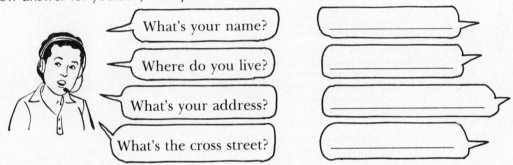

What's your name?	_____
Where do you live?	_____
What's your address?	_____
What's the cross street?	_____

Fire

If you have a fire in your house, or if you see a fire, call the operator or the Fire Department.

A *Practice this conversation.*

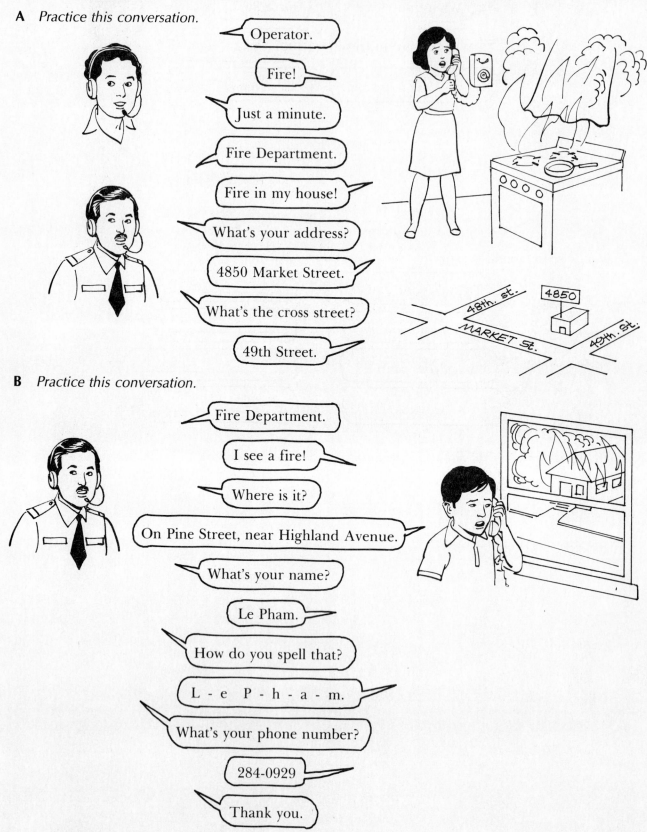

Operator.

Fire!

Just a minute.

Fire Department.

Fire in my house!

What's your address?

4850 Market Street.

What's the cross street?

49th Street.

B *Practice this conversation.*

Fire Department.

I see a fire!

Where is it?

On Pine Street, near Highland Avenue.

What's your name?

Le Pham.

How do you spell that?

L - e P - h - a - m.

What's your phone number?

284-0929

Thank you.

Ambulance

If you need an ambulance, call an ambulance or the Fire Department.

Practice this conversation.

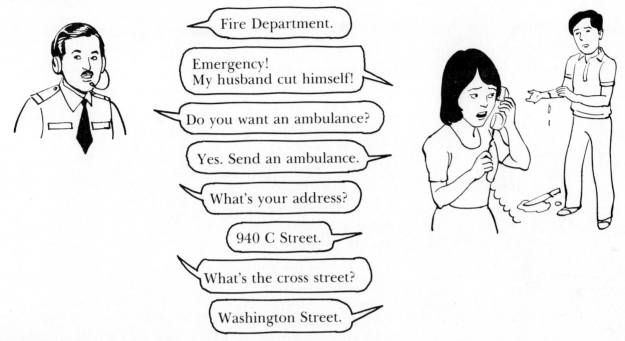

Fire Department.

Emergency!
My husband cut himself!

Do you want an ambulance?

Yes. Send an ambulance.

What's your address?

940 C Street.

What's the cross street?

Washington Street.

Now change the conversation and practice again.

My husband
My wife
My son
My daughter   . . .
My baby
My friend
Someone

. . cut himself
. . cut herself

. . is bleeding

. . fell down the stairs

. . is unconscious

. . can't breathe

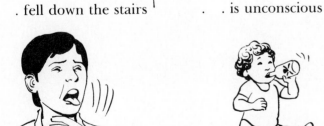

. . is choking

. . drank poison

. . is in labor
. . has labor pains

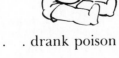

Police

If you see an accident, call the police.

A *Practice this conversation.*

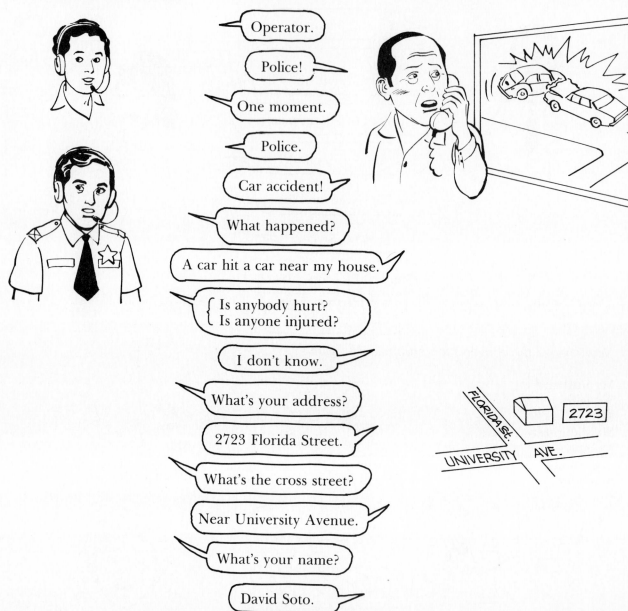

Operator.

Police!

One moment.

Police.

Car accident!

What happened?

A car hit a car near my house.

{ Is anybody hurt?
{ Is anyone injured?

I don't know.

What's your address?

2723 Florida Street.

What's the cross street?

Near University Avenue.

What's your name?

David Soto.

B *Practice this conversation.*

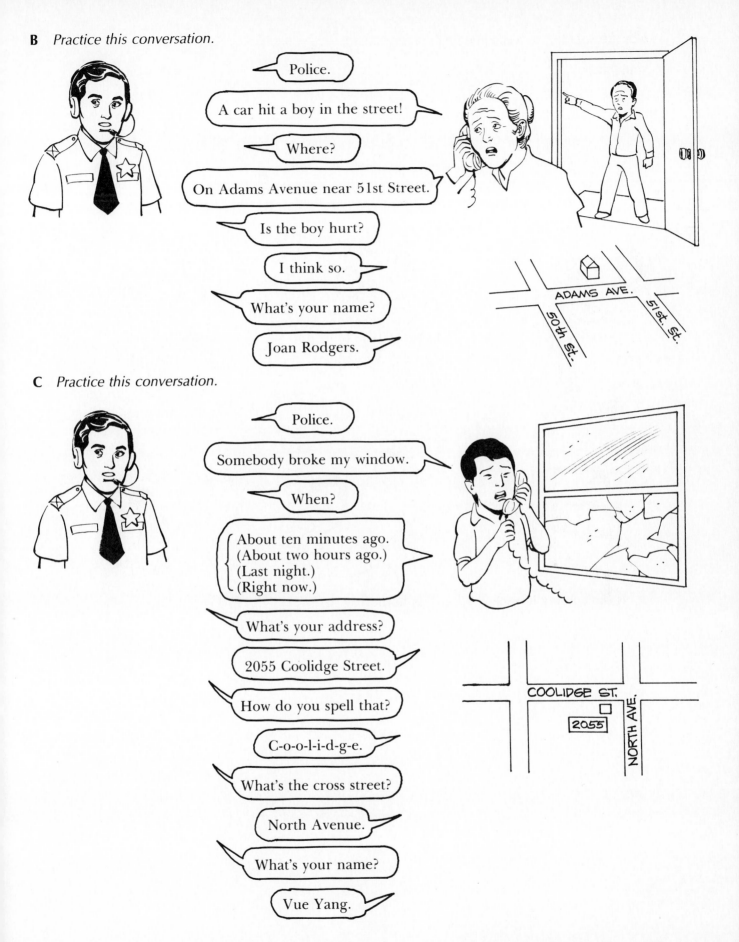

Police.

A car hit a boy in the street!

Where?

On Adams Avenue near 51st Street.

Is the boy hurt?

I think so.

What's your name?

Joan Rodgers.

ADAMS AVE.
50th St.
51st St.

C *Practice this conversation.*

Police.

Somebody broke my window.

When?

About ten minutes ago.
(About two hours ago.)
(Last night.)
(Right now.)

What's your address?

2055 Coolidge Street.

How do you spell that?

C-o-o-l-i-d-g-e.

What's the cross street?

North Avenue.

What's your name?

Vue Yang.

COOLIDGE ST.
NORTH AVE.
2055

Now change the conversation and practice again.

Somebody . . .

. . broke my window

. . robbed my house

. . robbed me

. . attacked me

. . stole my purse

. . is outside my house

. . is bothering me

. . is fighting

SELF-TEST

A *Write the conversation in the correct order.*

Sorry, she's not here.

I don't know. Who is this?

Hello.

This is Jim. I'll call again later.

What time will she come back?

Goodbye.

Hello. May I speak to Sue?

All right. Goodbye.

B *Fire in your house! Answer the questions.*

Fire in my house!

What's your address?

What's the cross street?

C *Answer these questions.*

1. There is a car accident! Who should you call? What should you say?

2. You see a fire. What will you do?

3. Your son can't breathe. What will you do?

4. Somebody broke your window. What will you do?

What Does He Look Like?

Practice this conversation with another student.

Somebody is outside my house!

What does he look like?

He's . . .

tall   short   fat   thin   young

old

He has . . .

long hair   short hair   a mustache   a beard

She has . . .

straight hair   wavy hair   curly hair

He's bald.

CLOTHING

Study these words.

shirt

sweater

blouse

purse

skirt

dress

pants

jacket

shoes

stockings

socks

coat

T-shirt

pajamas

shorts

underwear

hat

cap

belt

glasses

watch

ring

bracelet

necklace

earring

COLORS

Study these words.

red	orange	gray
blue	purple	gold
green	black	silver
yellow	brown	light blue
white	pink	dark blue

My Clothes

Study.

I'm wearing a yellow shirt.
I'm wearing blue pants.
I'm wearing black socks.
I'm wearing brown shoes.
What are you wearing?

I'm wearing a white sweater.
I'm wearing a pink blouse.
I'm wearing a gray skirt.
I'm wearing black shoes.
I'm wearing a silver necklace.
What are you wearing?

Fill in the blanks. Use "a" for singular.

1. I'm wearing _____.

2. I'm wearing _____.

3. I'm wearing _____.

4. I'm wearing _____.

5. I'm wearing _____.

6. I'm wearing _____.

Talking to the Police

A *Practice this conversation.*

Somebody robbed me!

What did he look like?

He's short and fat, with long curly hair.

How old is he?

I think he's about 25.

What was he wearing?

A dark blue T-shirt and brown pants.

B *Practice this conversation.*

What happened?

A man stole my purse.

When?

About ten minutes ago.

Where?

On the street in front of my house.

What did he look like?

He's tall and thin, and he has short black hair.

How old is he?

He's young, about 18.

What was he wearing?

A light brown jacket, blue pants, and white shoes.

SELF-TEST

A *Answer this question.*

What does he look like?

_____He's tall._____

_____

_____

_____

_____

_____

_____

_____

_____

B *Answer this question.*

What does she look like?

_____

_____

_____

_____

_____

_____

_____

_____

_____

_____

_____

listening and speaking

A *Listen to your teacher pronounce these words. Then listen again and repeat. Then listen to your teacher pronounce the key words below, and write under them the words that have the same sound in the same position. Check the word after you use it (√). Use some words twice (√) (√).*

light (√)   back ( ) ( )   speak ( )
call ( ) ( )   come ( )   live ( ) ( )
stole ( )   ring ( )   pants ( )

1	2	3	4	5	6
<u>c</u>ut	<u>l</u>ong	tal<u>k</u>	te<u>ll</u>	b<u>ig</u>	f<u>a</u>t
_____	<u>light</u>	_____	_____	_____	_____
_____	_____	_____	_____	_____	_____

Now think, and write one more word for each number.

_____   _____   _____   _____   _____   _____

B *Circle the cluster and pronounce.*

speak   small   skirt   sweater

straight   black   blue   blouse

brown   please   cross   green

dress

SAME PRONUNCIATION
no - know
for - four
to - two
our - hour
right - write
where - wear
there - their - they're

PRACTICE THESE WORDS

C *Your teacher will pronounce these words. Listen and repeat.*

```
 _  ´                        _  ´  _
po lice                      un con scious

´  _  _             ´  _  _  _                _  ´  _  _
am bu lance         o pe ra tor               e mer gen cy
ac  ci  dent
```

Now pronounce these words and write them above in the correct column.

Florida   underwear

Money and Banking

chapter two

COMPETENCIES:

1. Ask for and make change
2. Use a vending machine
3. Handle bills appropriately
4. Buy a money order
5. Cash a check
6. Open and use a savings account
7. Figure a monthly budget
8. Make knowledgeable choices about buying things
9. Make returns and exchanges of merchandise

ORIENTATION:

1. American currency
2. Vending machines
3. Bills
4. Use of checks and money orders
5. Banks: savings accounts, checking accounts, loans
6. Budgeting money
7. Good consumerism, comparative shopping
8. Return and exchange policies
9. Buying on credit

STRUCTURES:

1. Two-part verbs
2. Comparative forms of adjectives
3. Demonstrative adjectives

Teacher Notes and Suggestions

Page 23 1. Present using real money. Pass it around the class. Have students take out and count their pocket money.
2. Practice with equivalent amounts, for example,⑤+⑤=⑩. Practice adding money. Put circles on the board and have students figure out what the coins are, for example,◯◯◯◯ = 45¢ (㉕ ⑩ ⑤ ⑤).
3. Practice "change" dialogue by having students go around the classroom with money and ask for change.

Page 24 1. Explain what vending machines are, especially if students have not seen or used one. Take the class out to see a vending machine if possible. Explain how they work. Demonstrate Action Sequence, following the suggested procedure (see page *viii*).
2. Explain the picture of the vending machine at the bottom of the page. Use the example of putting in 50¢ and getting 15¢ change and contrast the pronunciation.

Page 25 1. Read the narrative; relate back to previous Action Sequence.
2. Point out the variations: "*put in* money" and "*put* money *in*."

Page 26 1. With many two-part verbs (verb and preposition) the preposition may come either immediately after the verb or at the end of the sentence. Practice these variations.
2. Examples and Action Sequence should be presented or practiced by actual demonstration.

Page 27 1. Introduce the topic by asking about students' rent. Do they get a bill? Do they get bills for their telephone and gas and electricity every month? Ask how they pay: Cash? Check? Money order? Explain what bills are; show examples if possible. Then read the page and discuss it. When reviewing the next day, have students bring their bills from home.
2. Point out the use of *have to*.

Page 28 1. To introduce the topic, ask again how students pay bills and where they buy money orders. Have a real money order as an example.
2. Present and practice the dialogue as suggested (see page *viii*).
3. Point out that the charge for a money order varies from place to place.
4. Explain that change is usually counted back to customers.
5. Draw a blank money order on the board and have students practice filling it out, perhaps using information from their own bills. Go through an entire sequence of receiving a bill, buying a money order, filling it out, and mailing it off to pay the bill.

Page 29 1. Introduce the topic by asking students if they receive checks they have to cash. Explain what checks and paychecks are. Show the class a real paycheck if possible. Ask how and where they cash their checks. Explain that it's often hard to cash a check and that there can be a varying charge for cashing one. Then practice the conversations as suggested.
2. Activity: After practicing this page, set up a bank situation in class. Teacher is the teller, students are customers assigned certain tasks: cash a check, buy a money order, pay a bill (a service some banks have). They line up as in a bank and are called to the "window" one by one. Later set up several "windows" and assign students as tellers and customers.

Page 30 Ask if any students have savings accounts now, and if any had accounts in their native country. Explain what a savings account is and how it works. Bring examples of bankbooks, deposit and withdrawal slips, and account statements. Set the situation of going to a bank to open a savings account, then present and practice the dialogue.

Page 31 Explain and demonstrate how a bank works. Each student puts money in your bank; some of this money you lend to one student who wants to buy a car but doesn't have enough money. He pays back money to your bank every month, but he has to pay back more than he borrowed because he is using the bank's money. Part of the extra money he pays to the bank the bank pays back to the students/investors because the bank is using their money. This money is interest, paid in proportion to the amount of money each person has in the bank. Explain why it's a good idea to have a savings account, as stated in the text. Explain in your own words the rest of the information on the page. Also ask if students know the location of banks near their house. Then refer to the text page. Read, practice, and discuss as suggested.

Page 33 Figuring a budget—thinking about a plan of income and expenses—may be new for many students. Explain in simple terms about the money we get and money we spend. Present a simplified example budget on the board and carry it through to where extra income that is not spent can be "savings." Then let students figure their own budget on the page. "Other Information" at the bottom is useful for students to be aware of.

Page 34 Look at the picture of the shopping center and point out different types of stores. In the students' native countries there are also different types of stores and stores with differing prices for their goods. Explain that they should shop around to find low prices in America just as they would in their native country. Talk about sales, advertising, return policy, how to make decisions about buying, and so on. Read and practice the page as suggested (see page *viii*) and discuss further.

Page 35 Compare classroom objects or students—e.g., one book is big, another is bigger; one student is tall, another is taller or shorter. Explain word form (*+er*), or—in the case of adjectives of more than one syllable not ending in *-y*—use of *more*. Practice several examples. Then refer to the page.

Page 36 Look at the picture at the top of the page. Set the situation and practice the conversation. Point out the use of comparatives; explain their formation, and practice further. Then have students look at the picture at the bottom of the page and take note of the information. In groups or individually, have them write a conversation similar to the one above, using the information given. Present good dialogues to the class and practice.

Pages 37 to 38
1. Relate to information from "Buying Things" that it is possible in most American stores to return or exchange merchandise. Ask students about the policy in their native country. Explain how it is done and that a receipt is usually necessary.
2. Role-play the first situation and practice, following the suggested procedure. Point out that *I'd like* is a polite way to say *I want*. Explain and demonstrate the idea of *too* (small, long, etc.). Also point out the use of *these* and *those;* compare with *this* and *that*.
3. In the second dialogue explain that there is often a special counter for returning merchandise.

Pages 38 to 39 Explain in your own words what buying on credit is and how it is done. Explain potential problems. Set the situation of the dialogue, then present and practice it. Then read Orientation Notes and discuss them. Explain the signs in the picture.

Money

Study.

 penny   one cent $ .01

 quarter   25 cents $ .25

 nickel   five cents $ .05

 half dollar   50 cents $ .50

 dime   ten cents $ .10

 dollar   100 cents $1.00

Practice.

Do you have change?

Do you have change for a quarter?

_____ a dollar?

_____ five dollars?

_____ a twenty?

Sorry, I don't.
I don't have change.

buying coffee from a vending machine

1. Take out your money.
2. Put the money in the machine.
3. Push the button.
4. The change comes down.
5. Take the change.
6. Put it in your pocket.
7. The cup comes down.
8. The coffee comes out.
9. Take out the cup of coffee.
10. Drink it.

Read.

In America there are machines that sell things. They are called *vending machines*. Most vending machines sell some kind of food or drink.

You put money in the machine, press a button, and the food comes out. You can put in quarters, dimes, or nickels—don't put in pennies. Some machines give change, but for some machines you must have *exact change*. Read the sign on the machine before you put your money in.

Study the signs. Which machines give change?

```
DEPOSIT  NICKELS
DIMES, OR  QUARTERS
_____

CHANGE  RETURNED
      BELOW
```

```
MACHINE DOES NOT
  GIVE CHANGE
```

```
EXACT  CHANGE  ONLY
_____
NO  CHANGE  RETURNED
```

```
NO CHANGE
WHEN  RED
LIGHT ON
```

If you see a light next to the thing you want, there is no more.

structure practice

Study.

Examples:

	I	II
1.	*Put in* your money.	*Put* your money *in*.
2.	*Take out* the cup.	*Take* the cup *out*.
3.	*Throw away* the cup.	*Throw* the cup *away*.

■ *action sequence* ➡

giving and following directions

Read and practice column I. Then change the sentences to the form in column II and practice them again.

I	II
1. *Take out* your notebook.	*Take* your notebook *out*.
2. Open your notebook.	Open your notebook.
3. *Pick up* your pencil.	_____
4. Write in your notebook.	_____
5. *Put down* your pencil.	_____
6. Close your notebook.	_____
7. *Put away* your notebook.	_____

I	II
1. *Turn on* the light.	_____
2. *Take out* your glasses.	_____
3. *Put on* your glasses.	_____
4. Read the book.	_____
5. *Take off* your glasses.	_____
6. *Put away* your glasses.	_____
7. *Turn off* the light.	_____

Now practice again with another student.

Read and discuss.

People in America have to pay bills every month. They have to pay rent and pay for their utilities and telephone. Some people also pay every month for their car and television.

You can pay your bills at the company office or sometimes at banks, or you can *mail* your *payment*. If you pay by mail, you have to send a *money order* or a *check*. Don't send cash in a letter. Send part of the bill with your payment, and keep the other part.

There is a *due date* on the bill. You have to pay the bill before this date. Always pay your bills *on time*. Don't pay late.

When you pay the rent or the bills, always keep the *receipts*. Put them in a drawer at home. If the company says you didn't pay, show the receipt.

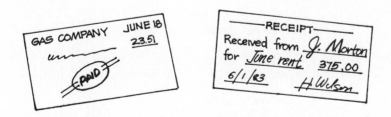

Buying a Money Order

Read.

You can buy a money order at a bank, at the post office, or at a supermarket. You have to pay a *charge* for the money order. Sometimes banks give free money orders if you have an *account* there.

Practice this conversation.

Clerk:	May I help you?
Woman:	Yes, I want a money order for $18.35.
Clerk:	Do you have an account here?
Woman:	No, I don't.
Clerk:	There's a 50¢ charge. That's $18.85.
Woman:	Here.

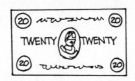

Clerk: Here's your money order for $18.35 and your change.

$$18.85 \left(+ \boxed{5¢} = \right) 18.90 \left(+ \boxed{10¢} = \right) 19.00 \left(+ \boxed{ONE \; ONE} = \right) 20.00$$

Thank you.

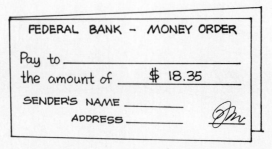

Cashing a Check

Read.

If you get money from a job or from the government, you don't get *cash.* They pay you by *check.* You have to take the check to a bank or maybe to a store and *cash* it. The bank will give you money for your check.

Sometimes banks won't cash your check because they don't know you. If you have an account at a bank, usually the bank will cash your check. Some places *charge* you for cashing a check.

A *Practice this conversation.*

Clerk: May I help you?

Man: I want to cash this check.

Clerk: Do you have an account here?

Man: No, I don't.

Clerk: I'm sorry. We can't cash your check if you don't have an account here.

Man: Where can I cash it?

Clerk: Try another bank or a supermarket.

B *Practice this conversation.*

Clerk: Next, please.

Man: Can you cash this check for me? I don't have an account here.

Clerk: There's a $2.00 charge. Do you have identification?

Man: Yes, here's my driver's license.
my ID card.
my I-94.
my green card.

Clerk: Please sign the back of the check.
—That's $237.60:
20–40–60–80–100; 20–40–60–80–200;
20–30–35–36–37 and 60 cents.
Minus the $2.00 charge . . . Thank you.

SIGN HERE
(ENDORSE)

Opening a Savings Account

Read and practice.

Anybody can open a savings account. You can start an account with only ten or twenty dollars. Go to the New Accounts desk at the bank.

Man:	I want to open a savings account.
Woman:	A *regular* savings account? (A *passbook* account?)
Man:	Yes.
Woman:	Do you have identification? I need to see two.
Man:	Yes. Here.
Woman:	Good. Do you want an *individual account* or a *joint account*?
Man:	A joint account—for me and my wife.
Woman:	All right. Please read and sign this paper, and take one home for your wife to sign.
Man:	OK. I'll send it back to you.
Woman:	How much do you want to put in the account?
Man:	Fifty dollars.
Woman:	Just a minute. I'll give you a *bankbook.*

Man:	Thank you.
Woman:	This is a *deposit slip.* Use it when you want to put money in your account. This is a *withdrawal slip.* Use it when you want to take money out of your account.
	Do you have any questions?
Man:	No. Thank you very much.

Orientation Notes: BANKS

Read and discuss.

A bank is a *business* that works with money. People put money in the bank and the bank *lends* the money to other people or to businesses.

Savings Account

Money you keep (save) in the bank is called a *savings account*. The bank gives you a bankbook or a passcard, and you can put money in or take money out when you want. The bank pays you *interest* on your money, about 5% a year.

It's a good idea to open a savings account because:

1. You can cash your checks.
2. Sometimes you can get free money orders.
3. The bank will pay you interest.
4. Maybe you can get a *loan* from the bank.
5. Your money is *safe*.

Checking Account

With a *checking account* you can write *checks* to pay your bills. You don't have to buy money orders.

At most banks you have to pay a little every month for your checking account, and sometimes you pay a little for every check you write.

Loans

If you want to buy a car or a house and you don't have enough money, sometimes you can *borrow* money from a bank (get a *loan*). You can get a loan if you have a good job and a savings account and if you always pay your bills on time. You have to pay the bank back a little every month. The bank charges you interest (about 18%) on your loan, so you have to pay back more than you borrowed.

What bank should you go to?

You can open an account at any bank, but most people go to a bank near their house or near work, because it is *convenient*—it's close and it's easy to use. Some people like to go to a bank that gives free money orders or free checking accounts. At a *savings and loan* you can usually get a little higher interest on the money in your savings account.

SELF-TEST

A   *Put these actions in order.*

_____ The cup comes down.

_____ Push the button.

_____ Take out the cup of coffee.

_____ Put the money in the machine.

_____ The coffee comes out.

_____ The change comes down.

B   *Fill in the blanks with the correct word(s).*

cash   money order   charge   receipts   savings account   bills   check

     1. Always pay your _____ on time.

     2. Always keep your _____ .

     3. You can open a _____ _____ at a bank.

     4. You can buy a _____ _____ at a bank.

     5. Sometimes banks will _____ you to _____ your _____ .

C   *Why is it a good idea to open a savings account?*

     1. _____

     2. _____

     3. _____

     4. _____

     5. _____

D   *Right or wrong?*

    _____ 1. You can use pennies in vending machines.

    _____ 2. All vending machines give change.

    _____ 3. You can pay bills by mail.

    _____ 4. You should not send cash in a letter.

    _____ 5. You need identification to buy a money order.

    _____ 6. Sometimes it's hard to cash a check.

    _____ 7. The bank will cash checks for everybody.

    _____ 8. You need a lot of money to open a savings account.

    _____ 9. The bank pays you interest on your savings.

    _____10. "Deposit" means "put in."

Read and discuss.

Working people get paid every month. Money we get is called *income*. We have to spend money, too. Things we spend money for are called *expenses*. If our income is more than our expenses, then we can *save* money.

A *plan* or *list* of our income and expenses is called a *budget*. Think about your income and expenses for one month and make a monthly budget for yourself.

INCOME	
1. Job	
2. Welfare	
3. Food stamps	
4. Other	
TOTAL	

EXPENSES	
1. Rent	
2. Food	
3. Bus	
4. Car	
5. Gasoline	
6. Telephone	
7. Utilities	
8. Clothing	
9. House supplies	
10. Health care	
11. Medicine	
12. Insurance	
13. Washing clothes	
14. Letters, stamps	
15. Fun	
16. Send to my family	
17. Other things	
TOTAL	

INCOME	
EXPENSES	—
SAVINGS	

OTHER INFORMATION	
Number of people in household	
Number of people employed	
Number of children under 18	

Read and discuss.

There are many different kinds of stores in America. Some stores sell food, some sell clothes, some sell furniture, some sell everything. Some stores have high prices, some have lower prices. Before you buy something expensive like a television or a stereo or a camera, go around to many different stores and find a low price. The price you see marked is the price you have to pay. You can't ask for a lower price.

Stores often have *sales* and sell things at special low prices. Watch for signs in the store windows or inside the store. Sometimes the newspapers tell you about sales.

Compare the prices.

There are many different kinds of televisions and cameras, from very cheap to very expensive. Which one should you buy? Think about what you need and how much money you have. Don't buy an expensive one if a cheaper one is good enough. Buy good *quality* if you can. Don't buy the cheap one if it's not good.

Don't buy something only because you see Americans have it or your friends have it. Save your money for something you really want.

structure practice

Study.

_____ + er

old

older

Examples:

					BUT:	
old	–	old<u>er</u>	happ<u>y</u>	–	happ<u>ier</u>	
young	–	young<u>er</u>	pretty	–	prett<u>ier</u>	expensive – <u>more</u> expensive
tall	–	tall<u>er</u>				beautiful – <u>more</u> beautiful
short	–	short<u>er</u>	far	–	farther	comfortable – <u>more</u> comfortable
close	–	clos<u>er</u>	good	–	better	etc.
big	–	big<u>ger</u>	bad	–	worse	

A *Answer the questions.*

Ted   Walter

1. Who is taller? _____
2. Who is older? _____
3. Who is younger? _____
4. Who is shorter? _____

Fill in the blanks.

5. Ted is _____ than Walter.
6. Ted is _____ than Walter.
7. Walter is _____ than Ted.
8. Walter is _____ than Ted.

B *Answer the questions.*

REX $ 12,000

1. Which car is bigger? _____
2. Which (one) is cheaper? _____
3. Which (one) is more expensive? _____
4. Which (one) is smaller? _____

Fill in the blanks.

5. The Sport is _____ than the Rex.
6. The Sport is _____ than the Rex.
7. The Rex is _____ than the Sport.
8. The Rex is _____ than the Sport.

SPORT $6200

Which One?

Read the conversation. Then practice with another student.

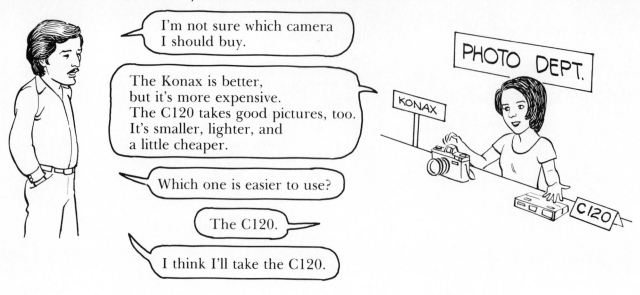

I'm not sure which camera I should buy.

The Konax is better, but it's more expensive. The C120 takes good pictures, too. It's smaller, lighter, and a little cheaper.

Which one is easier to use?

The C120.

I think I'll take the C120.

Now look at this picture and write a conversation similar to the one above.

Ride the X-10
- big
- strong
- comfortable
$85

SPRINT
- small
- light
- fast
$175

The X10 is _____

_____

The Sprint is _____

_____

Returns and Exchanges

You can return or exchange most things you buy in American stores, if you bought the wrong thing, or if it doesn't work, or if clothes don't fit, or if you want another color. Usually you need a receipt to return something.

Study.

near	far
this	that
these	those

A *Practice this conversation.*

> *Clerk:* May I help you?
>
> *Man:* Yes, I'd like to *exchange* these pants. They don't fit. They're too small (big/long/tight/loose).
>
> *Clerk:* Do you have the receipt?
>
> *Man:* Yes, here it is.
>
> *Clerk:* All right. Let me have those pants.
> You can look over there and find the right size. Then come back and I'll make the exchange.
>
> *Man:* Thank you.

B *Practice this conversation.*

Clerk: May I help you?

Man: I'd like to *return* this flash.

Clerk: Is there anything wrong with it?

Man: It doesn't work.

Clerk: Did you read the *instructions?*

Man: Yes, I did, and I put the flash on my camera, but it didn't flash. I think maybe it's the wrong one for my camera.

Clerk: Take it to that counter over there, please.

Man: Thank you.

Buying on Credit

Read and practice.

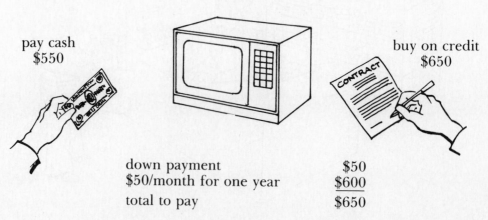

Dan goes to see his neighbor Tom. Tom has a big new color television.

Dan: Wow! You have a new TV! When did you get it?

Tom: I bought it last week.

Dan: Where did you buy it?

Tom: At Frank's TV Shop on Highland Avenue.

Dan: Was it expensive?

Tom: $550.

Dan: Did you pay cash?

Tom: No, I paid $50 down, and I'll pay $50 a month for one year.

pay cash
$550

buy on credit
$650

down payment		$50
$50/month for one year		$600
total to pay		$650

In America, if you don't have enough cash to buy something very expensive, you can often buy it *on credit*. Many people buy cars, televisions, and other things on credit. You pay a small part of the price in cash *(down payment)* and then you make *time payments (installments)* every month for one or two or more years. You have to pay an extra charge when you buy on credit, and you have to sign a *contract*.

Usually it's not a good idea to buy a lot of things on credit. It's more expensive than paying cash and every month you have to make big payments. If you don't pay, the company can take away the car or TV and you lose everything.

listening and speaking

A *Listen to your teacher pronounce these words. Then listen again and repeat. Then listen to your teacher pronounce the key words below, and write under them the words that have the same sound in the same position. Check the word after you use it (✓).*

sale ( )   young ( )   bought ( )   dime ( )
near ( )   did ( ) ( )   wrong ( ) ( )
paid ( )   here ( )   cent ( )

1	2	3	4	5	6
<u>d</u>ollar	<u>s</u>end	nee<u>d</u>	thi<u>ng</u>	t<u>a</u>ll	<u>year</u>

_____ _____ _____ _____ _____ _____

_____ _____ _____ _____ _____ _____

Now think, and write one more word for each number.

_____ _____ _____ _____ _____ _____

B *Circle the cluster and pronounce.*

slip small spend sport

special plan place price

press free credit close

throw

half / have fit / feet
safe / save slip / sleep

loose / lose sell / sale
close / close let / late
(near)

wash / watch
cash / catch

PRACTICE THESE WORDS

C *Your teacher will pronounce these words. Listen and repeat.*

ma chine   de po sit   re gu lar   in di vi du al
ac count
ex pense

Now pronounce these words and write them above in the correct column.

return   beautiful   instructions   exchange   everything

Work

chapter three

Teacher Notes and Suggestions

Page 45   1. Begin the chapter on work by talking about personal background. Ask several students about when they came to the United States, what they did in their country, when and where they were born, and so on. Point out the use of past tense in talking about the past.

   2. Tell students you will tell them the story of a man who came to live in the United States. Read Tony's story to the class (books closed) and ask comprehension questions; then, referring to the page, the class reads the story together and discusses it further.

   3. Students now write their own story, using Tony's story as a format. Help students use correct language. Students may want to write a fuller story of their experiences and should be encouraged to do so, though perhaps as a follow-up assignment.

   4. Using the information recorded in their story, students in pairs ask each other the questions at the bottom of the page.

Page 46   Have the class read the examples and discuss them. Students then each fill out the bottom for themselves, drawing a picture as well as they can. In some cases they can say, "I was a _____ ," in others, "I worked in/as a _____ ," or "I *(verb)*."

Page 47   This page outlines the rest of the chapter. Read and discuss it thoroughly. Explain that in this chapter the class will study about these three major points and that at the end the students will understand about working in America.

Page 48   Study the vocabulary as suggested (see page *viii*). Ask what jobs students may now have and discuss students' job expectations.

Page 49   Explain that students will answer the questions by referring to the jobs shown on the previous page and analyzing and categorizing them as required.

Page 50   1. Refer back to page 47 and remind the students of the three things that they need in order to get a good job. Explain what a skill is; give examples.

   2. Ask the students, "What can you do?" Make a list on the board, and include such things as *sing, cook, swim, take pictures,* and so on. Show the class that everybody can do something. Then have students practice in pairs and ask each other, "Can you _____ ?" answering as shown in the pictures.

   3. Look at the list again and ask students to think of which skills would be useful in jobs and what those jobs might be.

   4. Study the chart in Part B. Discuss the skills listed for each job. Then have the class discuss and write the skills needed for custodian (e.g., sweep floors, wash windows, clean rooms, cut grass, etc.).

Page 51   1. U.S. school systems differ from one city to another; teach the students about the system used in your area. Then compare the U.S. system to the systems used in the students' native countries.

   2. Before having the students fill in the form about their education, give an example on the blackboard. If their schooling was outside the United States, students need give for "name" and "location" only the level and the country. Form keys to the application form on page 59.

   3. Explain education as a continuing process that the students can pick up at their particular level and carry through as far as they like. Discuss students' educational and professional goals, and emphasize that they should be realistic.

Page 52   1. Introduce the topic of experience by reminding the students of three things necessary to get a good job: skill, education, and experience. Explain experience as "what you did before" and indicate that it can help students get a job in the United States. Then read about the experience of the man at the top of the page. Ask comprehension questions and discuss.

2. The time line in the center of the page shows graphically the man's experience over the years. Discuss and ask comprehension questions. Then use the time line and the information in the man's story to fill out the work history form below. Point out that such experience sections of forms usually start with the present job and go back.

3. Have the students think about their experience and make a time line for themselves.

Page 53

1. In reading the top paragraph, point out the use and meaning of present perfect tense.

2. Students fill out the forms for themselves. They should account for all their time, whether they were actually employed or not (e.g., 1982–1983 student; 1979–1982 refugee, etc.). Form keys to the application form on page 59.

3. After reading Orientation Notes, students should give three references such as teachers, counselors, community workers, sponsors, and the like.

Page 54

Structure: present perfect tense. Present and practice as suggested on page *viii*.

Pages 54 to 55

1. Present the questions orally first; have the class practice the questions and answers. After writing the answers, students practice again in pairs.

2. Practice the conversation in Part B as suggested on page *viii*. After final practice with the dialogue, student pairs may substitute their own information as answers and practice further.

Page 57

1. Discuss methods of finding a job. Inform the students of what community agencies (usually government agencies or ethnic service organizations) have job placement services they may use.

2. Using classified ads to locate jobs is a very difficult process and may not be appropriate for other than advanced level students.

Page 58

1. Point out that forms of all sorts are encountered throughout American society and people must be able to fill them out properly. Job application forms are especially difficult to fill out, even for Americans.

2. Discuss the information given at the bottom of the page and fill out the form. A similar section appears on the application form on page 59.

Page 59

Students should now be able to fill out the application form. Focus on it, explain it, and have the students fill it out a section at a time: Personal Data, Employment Desired, Education, and so on. Students can look back to keyed sections as references in filling out the form. Neatness should be required. Check the accuracy and completeness of the finished forms. Suggest that students keep the completed form and use it as a model and reference for filling out other forms in the future.

Page 60

Structure: Point out the use of *might* for possibility (= "maybe").

Pages 61 to 62

Present and practice as suggested on page *viii*. In the overall discussion go over the complete dialogue line by line and ask what is happening, what is being asked or brought up. For example, there is the introduction and handshake scene; the initial informal remarks; Tony's mentioning his evening studies, which could show him to be hard-working and eager to learn; Tony telling how he found out about the job; and so on. Ask the students to identify the lines in which Mr. Jensen asks about Tony's experience, his education, and his skill; have them identify the questions Tony asks about the job; have them find what he says that shows his confidence; have them consider why Mr. Jensen hired Tony.

Page 62

Structure: Point out use of *I'd/we'd like* as polite for *want*.

Page 63 You can use the practice interviews for simple pair practice or for a major class activity. After explaining the chart and asking comprehension questions, set up "companies" in different parts of the room, with secretaries, personnel managers, and application forms. Students apply for a job they would like to have, teacher seeing that applicants are fairly well distributed to the various companies. Applicants fill out applications and are interviewed. At end of the activity, ask various personnel managers who among the people they interviewed they would hire, and for what reasons.

Page 65 1. Details of paycheck deductions will require more explanation; you will need to explain what the U.S. Social Security and income tax systems are and how they work.
2. Explain that pay and benefits are different for every job and that applicants should ask about them in the job interview.

Page 68 to 70 These pages point out several possible problems in understanding directions and offer responses that will get the necessary clarification. Introduce the idea of asking for clarification, that it is necessary for good communication and that it is expected by employers. Present and demonstrate several examples. Then explain the various types of clarification presented on these pages, giving examples. Then read and follow the instructions, taking the exercises a section at a time.

Tony's Story

Read.

My name is Tony Parelli. I was born in Italy on August 11, 1950. My father was a salesman. I had four brothers and two sisters. We lived in Rome. I went to school ten years. After I finished school, I helped my father in his business for three years. Then I got a job in a construction company. I got married in 1975. I came to the United States in 1981.

Now write your own story.

_____ STORY
Write Your Name

_____

_____

_____

Draw Your Picture Here

_____

_____

_____

_____

Answer these questions and practice with another student.

1. When were you born?
2. Where were you born?
3. Did you come from a big family?
4. What did your father do?
5. What did your mother do?
6. Where did you live?
7. Is it a big city?
8. How many years did you go to school?
9. What did you do after you finished school?
10. Did you have many jobs?
11. When did you get married?
12. When did you leave your country?
13. Why did you leave your country?
14. When did you come to the United States?

What Did You Do in Your Country?

Read.

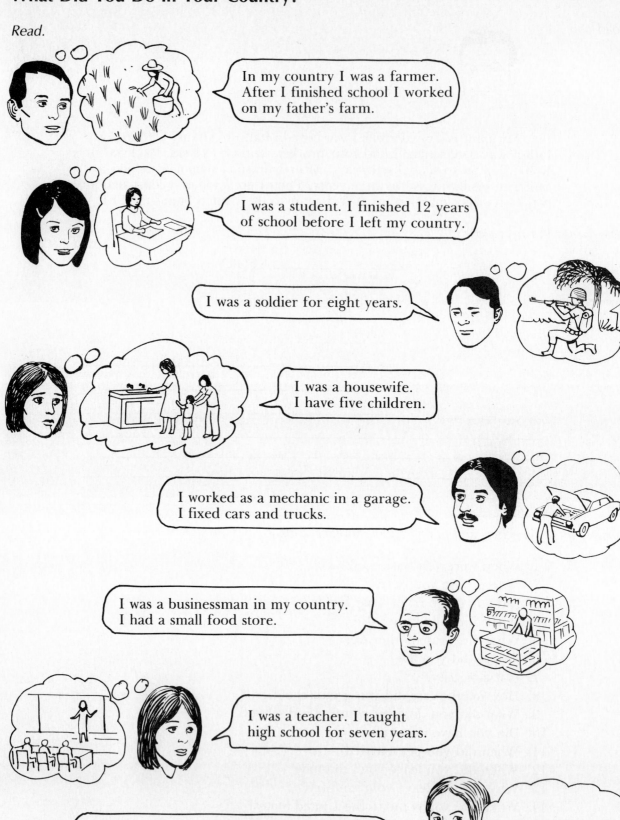

In my country I was a farmer. After I finished school I worked on my father's farm.

I was a student. I finished 12 years of school before I left my country.

I was a soldier for eight years.

I was a housewife. I have five children.

I worked as a mechanic in a garage. I fixed cars and trucks.

I was a businessman in my country. I had a small food store.

I was a teacher. I taught high school for seven years.

Read and discuss.

In America people need money to live. They get money from a job. Most people in America live in the city and have a job. Usually they work for a *company*. The company pays them for working.

What kinds of jobs are there?

There are many different kinds of jobs. Some people work in an office, some people work in a *factory,* and some people work outside. Some jobs have high pay, and some jobs have low pay.

What do you need to get a job?

To get a job, first you need to speak and understand English. Three other things you need are:

1. a *skill* (something you can do)
2. *education* (school)
3. *experience* (you worked before)

If you don't have a skill, education, or experience, you can get a job but the pay will probably be low and the work may be hard and long.

How can you find a job?

To find a job, you have to go to a company that needs workers. Maybe your friends know which companies need workers. Sometimes there are *community agencies* that can help you find a job.

When you go to a company to *apply* for a job, you have to fill out an *application form.* Then you will have an *interview.* If you're good, you can get the job.

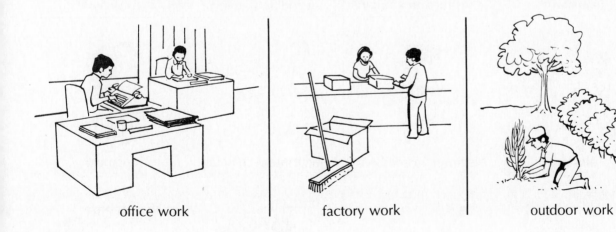

office work | factory work | outdoor work

JOBS

Study.

There are many different kinds of jobs in America. Your job is your *occupation* or *profession*.

office worker	factory worker	farmer	mechanic
store clerk	truck driver	waiter/waitress	policeman
tailor/dressmaker/ seamstress	construction worker	custodian (janitor)	soldier
salesman	electronic assembler	electronic technician	engineer
hairdresser	welder	watchman	repairman

What Kind of Job?

Answer these questions.

1. What did you do in your country? (What was your occupation?)

   _____

2. What kind of jobs do you like?

   _____   _____

   _____   _____

   _____   _____

3. What kinds of jobs can you do?

   _____   _____

   _____   _____

4. What kind of jobs *require:*

   a lot of education or training?   some education or training?   little education or training?

   _____   _____   _____

   _____   _____   _____

   _____   _____   _____

   _____   _____   _____

5. What kind of jobs require:

   hard physical work?   concentration?   working with people?

   _____   _____   _____

   _____   _____   _____

   _____   _____   _____

   _____   _____   _____

Orientation Notes: SKILLS

Read and discuss.

> A *skill* is something you can do: sew, type, drive, fix machines. To get a good job in America, you need some kind of skill. If you have a *special* skill, you can get a high-paying job. For some jobs you don't need a skill, but the pay is usually low, and sometimes the work is hard.
> You can learn a skill in school, or on a job (by *experience*). Studying about a skill is called *skill training*.

A   *Check (√) your skills on the list below.*

	good	fair	no
1. type			
2. file			
3. drive			
4. count money			
5. fill out forms			
6. sew			
7. cook			
8. take care of children			
9. clean houses			
10. paint			
11. wash dishes			
12. fix machines			

Now practice with another student, asking about the skills and answering as shown in the pictures above, according to the way the boxes are checked.

B   *Study the chart below. Then write the skills for the last job.*

Job	secretary	cashier	gas station attendant	repairman	custodian
Skills	type file	add count money use a cash register remember prices	pump gas check cars count money wash windows	use tools fix machines	

Orientation Notes: *EDUCATION*

Read and discuss.

To get a good job, you usually need a good education. Most Americans finish high school (12 years of school) before they look for a job. Many people go on to study at a university. If you don't have much education, you can get a job, but usually the pay will be low and it will be hard for you to move up in the company.

AMERICAN SCHOOLS

School	Age	Number of years	
(Kindergarten)	4	(1)	
Elementary school (primary, grammar)	5–11	6	8
		or	
Secondary school (high school)	12–18	6	4
		12	
University		4–5	

Fill in the information about your education.

Name of school	Location	No. years	Dates From – To
Elementary school			

American schools and companies are not sure about education in your country. If you want to move ahead, it's a good idea for you to go to school in America. Many states have adult schools (community colleges) where people who want to continue their education can go to study. You can study English in your free time, and you can study to get a high school diploma. Sometimes community colleges have skill training. Companies often have training programs for their employees.

Experience

Read.

What did you do before?
Tell me about your experience.

I went to school in Laos for eight years. I left school in 1963, and then I worked on my father's farm. In 1967 I got a job as a clerk in a store, and I worked there for three years. In 1970 I went into the Army, and I trained to be a mechanic. I got out in 1975 and I worked as a mechanic for four years. I came to the United States in 1979 and I studied English for one year. In 1980 I got a job in a shoe factory in Chicago.

1955	1963	1967	1970	1975	1979	1980	now (present)
student	farmer	clerk	soldier	mechanic	student	factory worker	

Look at the time line for this man. Then fill in the dates and positions. Start with the job he has now and go back.

EMPLOYER (company)	LOCATION (place) (address)	DATES (from–to)	POSITION (job)
ABC Shoe Company	Chicago	1980–present	factory worker
Chicago Adult School	Chicago	1979–1980	student
Downtown Garage	Laos		
Laotian Army	Laos		
Central Market	Laos		
Farm	Laos		

Orientation Notes: *WORK EXPERIENCE*

Read and discuss.

What you have done before is *experience*. If you had a job before, you have *work experience*. This will help you get a job. American *employers* like workers with experience, because they know the worker has had a job before and knows how to work.

> Where have you worked before?
> What experience have you had?

Fill in the information. Start with your present job.

WORK EXPERIENCE (EMPLOYMENT HISTORY)

Employer	Address	Dates	Position

If you never had a job before, or if you don't have work experience in the United States, it may be hard for you to get a good job. The employers are not sure about you—they don't know if you will be a good worker. Your first job will probably pay little, but later, after you have some experience, you can move up in your job, or you can change to a better job.

Sometimes American jobs are different from jobs in your country. A carpenter in America may not be the same as a carpenter in your country. Some employers think that a skill or experience in another country is not as good as in America. You need to get experience working in America.

Sometimes employers want to find out more about you. They want to talk to somebody who knows you well—your employer, your teacher, your counselor. These people we call *references*.

Fill in the three references for yourself.

REFERENCES

Name	Address	Telephone	Relationship

structure practice

Study.

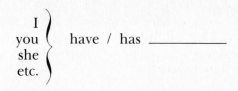

I
you } have / has _____
she
etc.

live - lived - *lived*   BUT:
work - worked - *worked*   be - was - *been*
study - studied - *studied*   go - went - *gone*
have - had - *had*   see - saw - *seen*
etc.   etc.*

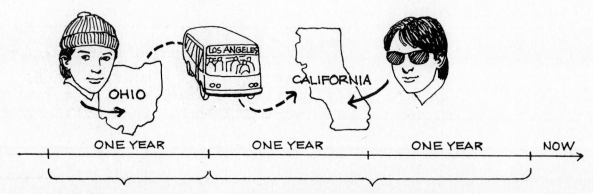

ONE YEAR   ONE YEAR   ONE YEAR   NOW

I lived in Ohio one year.   I *have lived* in California two years.
                                   (And I'm still living there now.)

Examples:

1. I *have lived* in California (for) two years.
2. I *have been* in the United States (for) three years.
3. I *have (I've) studied* English (for) nine months.
4. *I've had* 12 years of education.
5. I *have not (haven't) had* a job before in the United States.
6. I *haven't worked* in America before.

Questions	Short answers	
7. *Have* you *had* a job before in the United States?	-Yes, *I have.*	-No, I *haven't.*
8. *Have* you *worked* in America before?	-Yes, I *have.*	-No, I *haven't.*
9. How long *have* you *been* in the United States?		
10. How long *have* you *lived* in your apartment?		

A *Answer the questions. Give a short answer and a long answer.*

1. How long have you been in the United States?

```
months                                months.
years       I've been in the United States    years.
_____                              _____
```

*See Appendix.

2. How long have you lived in (your city) _____)?

_____ _____

3. How long have you studied English?

_____ _____

4. How long have you lived in your apartment?

_____ _____

5. How long have you been married?

_____ _____

6. Have you had a job before?

_____ _____

7. Have you worked in the United States?

_____ _____

8. How many years of education have you had?

_____ _____

Now practice these questions with another student.

B *Practice this conversation.*

What did you do in your country?

I was a dressmaker. I worked in a tailor shop.

How long did you work there?
How long did you do that?
How long were you a dressmaker?

Six years.

Have you worked before in the U.S.?

Yes, I have.

What are you doing now?

I work in a clothing factory.

How long have you worked there?

For two years.
Since _____.

SELF-TEST

A *Match the definitions.*

occupation	school
experience	something you can do
education	education in a skill
employer	job
skill	somebody who knows you well
training	what you have done before
reference	company

B *Answer the questions.*

1. What do you need to get a good job?

   a. _____

   b. _____

   c. _____

   d. _____

2. How can you learn a skill?

   a. _____

   b. _____

3. Where can you get more education or training?

   a. _____

   b. _____

C *True or false?*

_____ 1. Most Americans have a job.

_____ 2. If you don't have a skill, you can't get a job.

_____ 3. Your first job may have low pay.

_____ 4. You can learn a skill by experience on a job.

_____ 5. You can learn English only in school.

_____ 6. Americans usually finish high school.

_____ 7. You can go to school after you get a job.

_____ 8. Work experience can help you get a job.

Orientation Notes: *FINDING A JOB*

Read and discuss.

To find a job, you have to find a company or business that needs workers. Look for a company that has *openings* in jobs you can do.

How can you find a job?

1. Ask your friends.
   > Maybe their company has *job openings* or maybe they know about another company.

2. Look for signs.
   > Some factories put openings on a sign outside.

3. Go to a *community agency.*
   > Some agencies have a *job placement* office to help people find a job.

4. Read the newspaper.
   > Many companies put job openings in the newspaper. Look in the "Want Ads" in the back of the newspaper.

5. Go to a company and ask.
   > If you know a company that has jobs you can do, go in and ask if they have any openings.

When you go to a company to look for a job, go to the *Personnel Office.* Tell them you want to apply for a job.

You should apply at several companies at the same time. If you don't get one job, maybe you can get another one.

Read and discuss.

Every company has an *application form* for people who are looking for a job. You have to fill one out. The company will read it and find out something about you.

Print clearly on the form. Use a pen. Fill out everything on the form. If you don't understand something, ask the secretary. If you want, you can take the form and fill it out at home.

Application forms are very difficult. Every company has a different form, but usually the forms ask for the same information.

Application forms ask about:

1. Personal information (personal data) (name, address, Social Security number . . .)
2. Education
3. Work experience (employment history)
4. Skills
5. References
6. The job you want:
   What job are you applying for? (position desired)
   When do you want to work? (work preferences)
   When can you start? (availability)

I want to apply for a factory worker job.
I can work any time.
I want full-time work.
I can start *now*.

Fill out the form for this man.

POSITION DESIRED	WORK PREFERENCES		AVAILABILITY
	☐ full time ☐ day shift ☐ part time ☐ night shift ☐ swing shift		

Practice Job Application Form

Fill out.

BEST BOX COMPANY • APPLICATION FOR EMPLOYMENT				
Please Print PERSONAL DATA		Social Security Number		
Last Name	First Name	Middle Initial	Maiden Name	Marital Status
Present Address	City	State	Zip Code	Telephone
Permanent Address	City	State	Zip Code	Telephone

EMPLOYMENT DESIRED
Position

Work Preferences ☐ day shift ☐ night shift ☐ swing shift
☐ full time
☐ part time

Availability

see p. 58

Have you ever applied here before?   When?   Referred by:

EDUCATION Name of School	Location	No. Years	Dates: From – To

see p. 51

EMPLOYMENT HISTORY (Start with your present job)

Employer	Address	Dates	Position

May we contact your present employer?   Mgr's Name   Phone

see p. 53

SKILLS   Special Skills   Driver's License   Yes ☐   No ☐

Certificates Held   Foreign Languages Spoken

Organizations, Clubs

see p. 50

REFERENCES   List three people who know you well.

Name	Address	Telephone	Relationship

see p. 53

In case of emergency notify:

Name   Address   Telephone

DATE   SIGNATURE

Read and discuss.

After you fill out an application at a company, they might want to talk to you (*interview* you). Many people apply for a job and the company wants to find the best person.

At a job interview the personnel manager talks to you about yourself and about the job. He asks you about your skills, your experience, and your education. He tells you about the job—about the work, the *hours,* the *pay,* the *benefits (insurance, vacation, sick leave).* He also wants to know if you speak and understand English.

If the manager wants to give you a job, he will tell you he'll *hire* you. If he's not sure, he might say, "Thank you, we'll call you." Maybe he'll call you, maybe he won't.

In the interview you should:

1. Shake hands with the manager.
2. Look at the manager in the eye when you're talking.
3. Talk about yourself and what you can do; you have to "sell yourself."
4. Listen carefully.
5. Ask questions about the job (but not only about pay and benefits).
6. Have *confidence.*

Tony's Interview

Read and practice this conversation.

Jerry told Tony about an opening at Best Box Company for a factory worker. Tony went to the Personnel Office and filled out an application form. Then he waited to see the personnel manager.

The personnel manager, Mr. Jensen, came in to talk to Tony. They shook hands.

Mr. Parelli?

I'm Bob Jensen.

Please come into my office.

Yes.

Tony Parelli.

They went into Mr. Jensen's office.

Mr. Jensen:	Have a seat. . . . So you're from Italy?
Tony:	Yes, I've been in America only six months.
Mr. Jensen:	Really? Your English is very good.
Tony:	Thanks, I'm trying. I study English at night.
Mr. Jensen:	Very good. . . . And what job are you applying for?
Tony:	Factory worker. My friend Jerry Morton told me you have an opening.
Mr. Jensen:	Yes, that's right. Have you worked in a factory before?
Tony:	No, I haven't, but I'm good with my hands and I learn fast.
Mr. Jensen:	What did you do in your country?
Tony:	I was a foreman for a construction company for five years.
Mr. Jensen:	How much education have you had?
Tony:	Ten years.
Mr. Jensen:	Any special training or skills?
Tony:	Yes, in using tools and equipment for my job.

Mr. Jensen:	Mm-hmm. . . . Well, I need someone to work in the assembly room at the cuttirg machine. You work with three or four other people cutting paper for boxes. Are you good around machines?
Tony:	Oh, yes. I'm sure I can do the job. Is it full time?
Mr. Jensen:	Yes. The hours are 7:00 A.M. to 4:00 P.M. The job pays $3.65 to start, with a raise after six months if you're doing well.
Tony:	That's fine. Is there any training available?
Mr. Jensen:	The other workers will train you for this job. Later we'll train you to use other machines. Do you have any other questions?
Tony:	Yes. Can you tell me about the benefits?
Mr. Jensen:	We have a good insurance plan for you, you get two weeks vacation after you've worked one year, and you get six sick days a year.
Tony:	Fine. What about layoffs?
Mr. Jensen:	That should be no problem. We haven't had any layoffs here in two years. In fact, we'd like you to work overtime once in a while on Saturdays.
Tony:	Sure. That's all right.
Mr. Jensen:	Well, what do you think? Are you interested in the job?
Tony:	Yes, very much.
Mr. Jensen:	Good. I'd like to hire you. Can you start on Monday?
Tony:	Sure.
Mr. Jensen:	Fine. Stop at the desk and the secretary will have some more papers for you to fill out. Thanks for coming in, and good luck.
Tony:	Thank you very much, Mr. Jensen. Goodbye.

Practice Interview

Look at these jobs. Work with other students and have practice interviews. Some students will be personnel managers, and other students will apply for jobs. Use the sample questions below and think of more. You can make up answers about the job.

Employer	Opening	Salary	Hours
1. Best Box Company	factory worker	3.65/hr.	7:00 A.M.–3:30 P.M.
2. King Drug Store	cashier	3.95/hr.	6:00 P.M.–10:00 P.M.
3. Dave's Garage	assistant mechanic	5.00–6.00/hr.	8:00 A.M.–5:00 P.M.
4. Downtown Coffee Shop	dishwasher	3.65/hr.	4:00 P.M.–12:00 A.M.
5. Top Electronics Corp.	assembler	3.65–3.90/hr.	12:00 P.M.–8:45 P.M.
6. City schools	bilingual teacher aide	4.50/hr.	8:00 A.M.–4:00 P.M.
7. Cozy Motel	housekeeper	3.85/hr.	6:00 A.M.–3:00 P.M.
8. Oakwood Day Care Center	child care worker	4.00/hr.	6:00 A.M.–12:00 P.M.

Questions

1. What job are you applying for?

2. Where are you from?

3. How long have you been in the United States?

4. Have you worked before in the United States?

5. What did you do in your country?

6. Do you have any skills?

7. How much education did you have? (How many years did you go to school?)

8. Are you going to school now?

9. What do you know about this kind of work?

10. How did you find out about the job?

11. Do you think you can do the job? Why?

12. Do you have any questions about the job?

Read and discuss.

Work

1. You have to work. Your *supervisor (manager, foreman, boss)* will tell you what to do. If you don't know enough about the work, the company will train you.
2. Your work must be good. If your work isn't good, or if you work too slowly, the supervisor will talk to you.

Hours

1. *Full-time* workers work 40 hours a week. Usually they work eight hours a day, five days a week, Monday to Friday. If you work more than 40 hours a week, or more than eight hours a day, that is *overtime*.
2. *Part-time* work is less than 40 hours a week.
3. Workers get a half hour or sometimes one hour for lunch, usually without pay.
4. Workers usually take a short *break* in the morning and in the afternoon.

Shifts

Usually you work from 8:00 A.M. to 4:30 or 5:00 P.M. Big companies can have two or three *shifts*.

1. Day shift: 8:00 A.M. to 5:00 P.M.
2. Swing shift: 12:00 P.M. to 8:00 P.M.
3. Night shift: 4:00 P.M. to 12:00 A.M.

Sometimes there is a shift from 12:00 A.M. to 8:00 A.M.

Rules

1. You have to come to work every day, and you have to come on time. If you are going to be late or absent, you have to call the office.
2. Most jobs have a *time card* or *time sheet* that workers use every day. This tells the company if you're late or absent.
3. Some jobs have special rules for using tools, cleaning up, and so on.

Unions

For some jobs you have to *join* a *union*. A union is an organization (group) of workers who have the same job; for example, there is a plumbers union and an electricians union. The union talks to the company for the workers about their working conditions, pay, and benefits. Workers have to pay *dues* to the union every month. It's often hard to get into a union.

Read and discuss.

Pay

1. Workers are usually paid *by the hour* ($_____ per hour). The law says that the *minimum wage* (lowest pay) you can make is $_____ an hour. If you work overtime, you get one and a half times your regular pay.
2. Some workers get paid every week, some every two weeks, some every month. You get paid by check, not cash.
3. After you have worked about six months, you can get a *raise.* Sometimes you have to ask for a raise.
4. Companies take out money from the *employees'* paychecks for *taxes* and *Social Security.* Money they take out is called *deductions.* Every year you have to pay *income tax* to the government on your pay.

Benefits (mostly for full-time workers)

1. *Insurance.* Companies often have a health insurance plan for the employees. Sometimes the company pays for your insurance, sometimes you pay all or half. Sometimes the insurance is only for you, and you have to pay more for your family.
2. *Vacation.* You usually get one or two weeks vacation a year, when you don't work and still get paid. You can take your vacation after you have worked one year.
3. *Sick leave.* You usually get five to ten days a year for sick leave. If you're sick, you can stay home and still get paid.
4. *Paid holidays.* You usually get paid on big holidays when your company is closed.
5. *Unemployment insurance.* You can usually get some money from the government if you lose your job or if you are *laid off* (the company tells you to stay home without pay because they don't have enough work to do).

Experience

Working gives you experience. You can learn from your experience, and it will help you get other jobs.

Orientation Notes: *SOME IDEAS ABOUT WORKING*

Read and discuss.

If you're a good worker, your employer will like you. You can get a raise or you can *move up* to a higher position, and you can get a good reference for your next job.

To be a good worker, you should:

1. Go to work *on time*. Don't be late. Don't be absent a lot. If you are going to be late, or if you can't go to work, call in to the office.
2. Work hard. Don't be lazy.
3. Work carefully. Always do your best.
4. Ask questions if you don't understand or if you're not sure.
5. Learn everything you can. Ask questions. Watch other people work.
6. Be friendly. *Get along* with everybody. Be nice to the other workers. Say hello to them. Talk to them. Smile at them. Be clean and neat.

If you have a problem, or if you're not happy about something at work, tell your boss. Maybe he can do something about it.

If you don't like your job, or if you don't move up, or if the pay is too low, or if you get laid off, you can *quit* (leave) and find another job. You should tell your employer two weeks before you want to leave. It's good to have experience in many jobs, but don't leave jobs too quickly. Other employers might not want to hire you if they think you will leave soon.

If you're a bad worker, the company can *fire* you. Then it might be hard for you to get another job, because you will have a bad reference.

SELF-TEST

A

The job pays $3.80 to start. The hours are 8:00 A.M. to 4:30 P.M. Monday through Friday, with a half-hour lunch. Your job is to pack lamps in boxes. The supervisor will show you what to do. You can get a raise after six months if you're working well. You get paid every two weeks. You get one week vacation and eight days sick leave a year. We have an insurance plan, too.

Answer these questions about the job.

1. What's the pay?

_____

2. What are the hours?

_____

3. Is it a full-time job?

_____

4. What do you have to do?

_____

5. Who will train you?

_____

6. When can you get a raise?

_____

7. When do you get paid?

_____

8. What are the benefits?

_____

B *Read the sentences and write "good" or "bad."*

_____ 1. I'm a careful worker.

_____ 2. Sometimes I come late to work.

_____ 3. I call the boss when I can't come to work.

_____ 4. I didn't feel like working, so I stayed home and took a sick day.

_____ 5. I didn't understand, so I asked the boss to explain again.

_____ 6. I needed some tools at home, so I took some from the drawer at work.

Making Sure

Study.

Sometimes you don't understand when people tell you things. You have to make sure you understand everything, or you might do the wrong thing. What should you do? What can you say?

Study each section. Follow the examples and write. Practice each section with another student after you finish.

A *If you don't understand anything, you can say:*

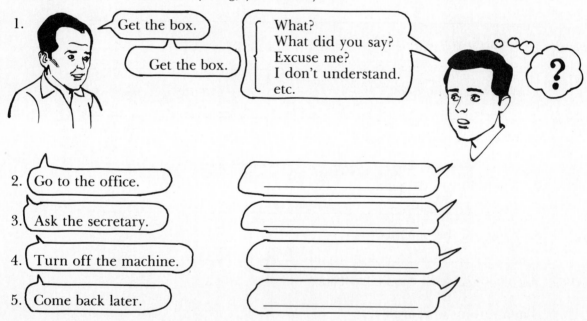

1. Get the box.

    Get the box.

    What?
    What did you say?
    Excuse me?
    I don't understand.
    etc.

2. Go to the office. _____

3. Ask the secretary. _____

4. Turn off the machine. _____

5. Come back later. _____

B *If you don't understand part, you can say:*

1. Get the box.
   The box.

   Get what?

   GET ___?

2. Go to the office.

3. Ask the secretary.

4. Turn off the machine.

5. Come back later.

C *If you think you understand but you're not sure, you can say:*

1. Get the box.
   Yes.
   Yeah.
   That's right.
   Uh-huh.
   etc.

   Get the box?
   The box?

2. Go to the office.

3. Ask the secretary.

4. Turn off the machine.

5. Come back later.

Work   **69**

D *If you understand but you need more information, you can say:*

1. Get the box.

   The big one.

   Which box?
   Which one?
   This one?
   That one?
   The big one?
   The small one?
   The big one or
       the small one?
   What size?
   Which size?
       etc.

2. Go to the office.

   _____

   Which one? The main office or the department office?

   MAIN OFFICE
   DEPT. ?

3. Ask the secretary.

   _____

   _____

   GLORIA   ?   JANET

4. Turn off the machine.

   _____

   _____

   _____

   GRINDER   ?   SANDER

5. Come back later.

   _____

   _____

listening and speaking

A *Listen to your teacher pronounce these words. Then listen again and repeat. Then listen to your teacher pronounce the key words below, and write under them the words that have the same sound in the same position. Check the word after you use it.*

sign ( )   join ( ) ( )   quit ( )   neat ( )
most ( )   pump ( )   job ( )
quickly ( )   know ( ) ( )   some ( )

1	2	3	4	5	6
janitor	question	never	line	go	luck

_____ _____ _____ _____ _____ _____

_____ _____ _____ _____ _____ _____

Now think, and write one more word for each number.

_____ _____ _____ _____ _____ _____

B *Change the first letter and make new words. Then pronounce them.*

1. day
2. p _____
3. s _____
4. m _____
5. pl _____
6. st _____
7. w _____
8. spr _____

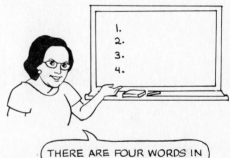

THERE ARE FOUR WORDS IN THIS UNIT THAT END IN **X**. CAN YOU FIND THEM?

C *Your teacher will pronounce these words. Listen and repeat.*

_ ´ _	´ _ _	_ _ ´	_ _ ´ _
me cha nic	com pa ny	en gi neer	e du ca tion
po lice man	fac to ry		
em plo yer	ja ni tor		
va ca tion	o pe ning		
as sem bly	be ne fits		

_ ´ _ _	´ _ _ _
cus to di an	se cre ta ry

Now pronounce these words and write them above in the correct column.

interview   remember   profession   supervisor   overtime   application
personnel   equipment   community   hairdresser

Driving

chapter four

COMPETENCIES:
1. Fill out a simple driver's license application
2. Recognize road signs and signals
3. Take a written driver's test
4. Follow instructions on a driving test
5. Report and describe an accident

ORIENTATION:
1. Driver licensing and testing procedures
2. Basic rules of the road
3. Traffic ticketing
4. Considerations in buying a car

STRUCTURES:
1. Impersonal expressions
2. Past continuous

Teacher Notes and Suggestions

Page 75 1. Driver licensing requirements and procedures as well as traffic regulations vary from state to state. Alter or supplement the information in this unit as necessary according to your local laws.

      2. Introduce the chapter by asking how many students have cars, how many have driver's licenses, how many want to get a license or a car. Ask students how they think people get around in America; they have probably noticed that most people have cars. Later they will probably also have a car. This chapter will not teach them how to drive but will tell them how they can get a license and what they should know about driving. Ask students who have licenses how they got them, where they applied, how they learned the rules. Discuss in class.

Page 76 Class fills out the form section by section as it is explained to them.

Page 77 Present and practice as suggested on page *viii*. Show the students a real car if possible.

Page 78 Present and practice Action Sequence as suggested on page *viii*.

Pages 79 Put the signs on larger visuals for class practice.
to 81

Pages 83 Explain these basic rules of the road. Many of the situations should be acted out,
to 85 particularly number 11, right-of-way. Have the students take positions of vehicles and act out the various situations.

Page 87 Structure: impersonal expressions. Give several examples orally first and explain the structures before doing the exercises.

Pages 88 1. Introduce the topic in your own words; ask if any students have ever gotten
to 89   traffic tickets. Have them explain the circumstances and outcome. Relate back to the topic, then read, explain, and discuss the page section by section.

      2. Put the signs on larger visuals for class practice.

Page 90 Review the licensing procedure and explain about the written test in your own words. Explain the structure of multiple choice tests and give some simple examples for practice before doing the page.

Pages 91 1. Role-play the situation with a student. Sit in chairs side by side; teacher/
to 92   examiner tells the student/driver to perform the steps in the Action Sequence. Then demonstrate the steps in front of the class and practice the sequence as suggested on page *viii*. Finish with student pair practice of a test situation, as preparation for a practice driving test.

      2. Activity: Practice the driving test. This may be done in pairs or as follows: Assign several good students to be driving examiners. They will give the driving test to other students and should understand the testing procedure well and be able to give driving directions as in the Action Sequence. Study the Score Sheet in class. Then give the names of several student "applicants" to each examiner, who will call them one by one for testing. The examiner takes the applicant's form and fills out the top, then gives the test, grading the applicant's performance. After marking "pass" or "fail," the examiner explains to the applicant what was done wrong. Go around the class monitoring testing operations. The process continues until all the students have been tested.

Page 93 Structure: past continuous. Present some example situations orally first; explain, contrasting to past tense, then practice as suggested on page *viii*. Then do the exercises on the next page.

Pages 95
to 96

1. Remind the students that drivers should call their insurance company after they are involved in an accident. The dialogue provides an example of such a call.

2. The class should study the picture at the bottom of page 96 and then describe the accident situation to the insurance company, using past continuous tense where appropriate. Students can then act out the situation in class.

Page 97

Ask how many students have cars, and how many would like to buy a car. Ask what kinds of cars they have or would like to have—for example, what make, whether it's big or small, new or used—and why. Ask where they bought the car, from whom. Then read and discuss the page. Ask students to explain the situation shown in the pictures at the bottom. Discuss their answers to the question. They should say that the man should:

1. Check the condition of the car.
2. Make sure he likes the car.
3. Compare it to other cars.
4. Get a lower price.

Orientation Notes: DRIVING

Read and discuss.

In America it's necessary to have a car. Most people know how to drive and have a car.

Americans usually learn how to drive in high school or from their family. If you want to learn how to drive, maybe a relative or friend can teach you. It's not hard. You also have to learn the *traffic laws* of your state. Then you can take a test and get a *driver's license*.

Getting a license

First go to the Motor Vehicle Department office. Get a Driver's Handbook and study it. When you know the traffic laws, you can take a test to get an *instruction permit* (learner's permit). With this permit you can practice driving on the road (with a licensed driver sitting next to you).

To get an instruction permit, usually you need to:

1. Fill out an application
2. Pay a *fee*
3. Take three tests:
   a. Eye test
   b. Written traffic law test
   c. Road sign test

If you pass the tests, you can practice driving. Later you can come back and take one more test: a driving test. If you pass this test, you can get a driver's license. They will give you a *temporary* license and later they'll send you your driver's license in the mail. If you *fail* the test, you can take it again later.

Your license *expires* after three or four years, and then you have to renew it.

EXPIRES 1988 x *Jerry Morton*

Applying for a License

Fill out this practice form.

DEPARTMENT OF MOTOR VEHICLES

Application Form

Check what you are applying for:

Driver's ☐   Instruction ☐   Identification Card: Regular ☐
License   Permit   Senior Citizen ☐
                                                                              (age 62 or over)

Class: ☐ 3   (Basic License)   ☐ 4   (Motorcycle)   ☐ 1   ☐ 2

Information Sheet

Please print carefully

Driver's license number or identification card number (if any)_____

Print complete name_____
                        first   middle   last

Mailing address_____ Apt. No.____

City_____ Zip Code_____

Sex_____ Color Hair_____ Color Eyes_____ Height_____ Weight_____

Birth Date_____
         Month   Day   Year

(Enter residence address if different from mailing address.)

Residence Address_____

City_____ Zip Code_____

-Have you applied in this state for a driver's license, instruction permit, or identification
   card within the past 12 months? (Circle which one you applied for.)   Yes ☐   No ☐

-Have you ever had a driver's license in this state?   Yes ☐   No ☐

-Have you ever had an identification card in this state?   Yes ☐   No ☐

If YES to any of the above, print year of expiration _____

PARTS OF A CAR

Study these words.

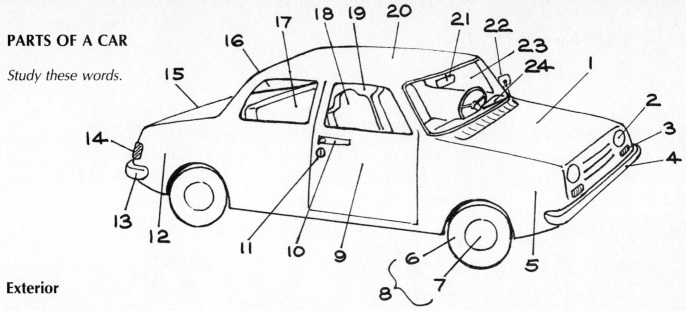

Exterior

1. hood
2. headlight
3. turn signal light
4. (front) bumper
5. (front) fender
6. tire
7. hubcap
8. wheel
9. door

10. door handle
11. lock
12. (rear) fender
13. (rear) bumper
14. tail light (and brake light and rear turn signal light)
15. trunk
16. rear window

17. back seat
18. front seat
19. window
20. roof
21. rear view mirror
22. side mirror
23. windshield
24. windshield wipers

Interior

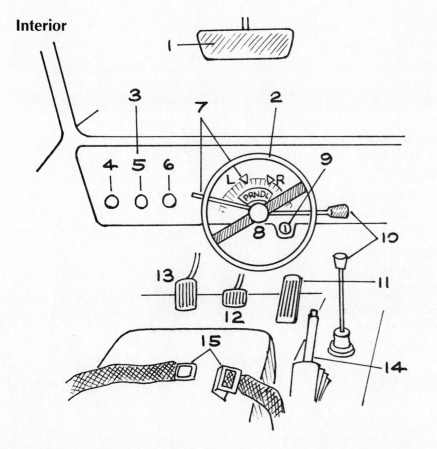

1. rear view mirror
2. steering wheel
3. dashboard
4. lights
5. wipers
6. emergency flasher
7. turn signal
8. horn
9. ignition
10. gearshift
11. gas pedal (accelerator)
12. brake
13. clutch
14. hand brake
15. seat belt

The Gearshift

Read and discuss.

When you drive a car you have to change *(shift)* the *gears.* Cars usually have 3 or 4 forward gears and one reverse gear. The gears change inside the *transmission.*

There are two kinds of transmissions: *standard* (manual, stick, 3-speed, 4-speed), and *automatic.* Automatic is easier to drive than standard, but it usually uses more gas.

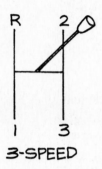

3-SPEED

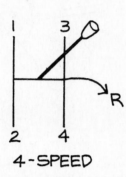

4-SPEED

manual transmission

PARK REVERSE NEUTRAL DRIVE LOW(1,2)

P R N D L

automatic transmission

■ *action sequence* ➡

driving a car

1. Take out your key.
2. Unlock the door.
3. Open the door.
4. Get in and close the door.
5. Fasten your seat belt.
6. (Push in the clutch.)
7. (Put the gearshift in neutral.)
8. Put the key in the ignition.
9. Push the accelerator (gas pedal).
10. Turn the key and start the engine.
11. Release the hand brake.
12. Switch on the turn signal.
13. Look in the rear view mirror.
14. Turn and look behind you.
15. Put the car in first gear./Put the car in DRIVE.
16. Pull out and drive away.

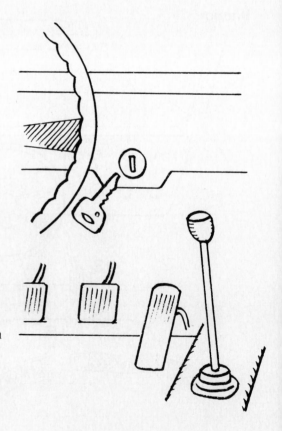

TURNS

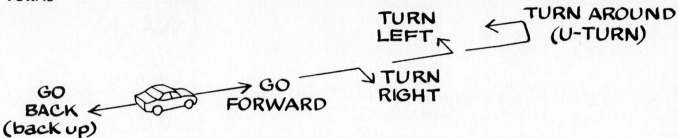

GO
BACK
(back up)

GO
FORWARD

TURN
RIGHT

TURN
LEFT

TURN AROUND
(U-TURN)

HAND SIGNALS

LEFT TURN

RIGHT TURN

SLOW OR STOP

TURN SIGNS

1

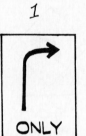

ONLY

2

ONLY

3

ON LEFT
ARROW
ONLY

4

DO NOT
ENTER

5

NO
TURN
ON RED

6

NO RIGHT
TURN

7

NO LEFT
TURN

8

NO U
TURN

9

WRONG
WAY

10

NO
TURNS

TRAFFIC SIGNAL LIGHTS

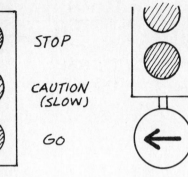

RED — STOP

YELLOW — CAUTION (SLOW)

GREEN — GO

stoplight
signal light
traffic light
traffic signal

turn arrow

WALK
DON'T WALK

WALK
WAIT

ROAD SIGNS

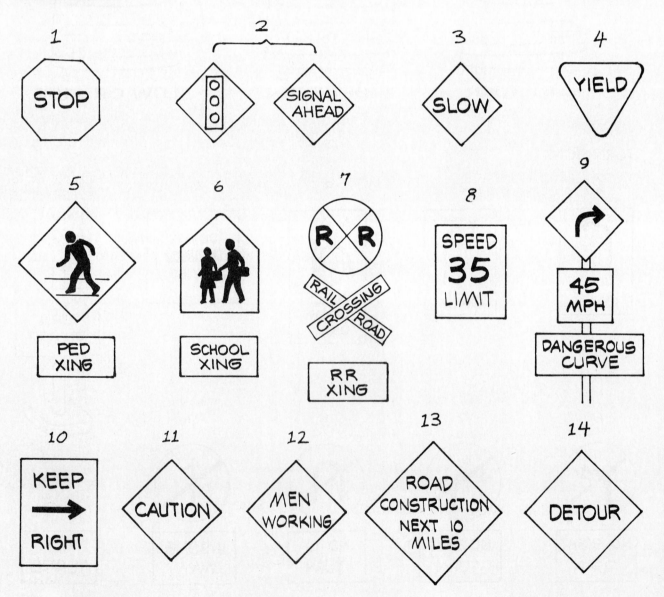

1 STOP

2 SIGNAL AHEAD

3 SLOW

4 YIELD

5 PED XING

6 SCHOOL XING

7 RR — RAIL CROSSING ROAD — RR XING

8 SPEED 35 LIMIT

9 45 MPH — DANGEROUS CURVE

10 KEEP RIGHT

11 CAUTION

12 MEN WORKING

13 ROAD CONSTRUCTION NEXT 10 MILES

14 DETOUR

ROADS

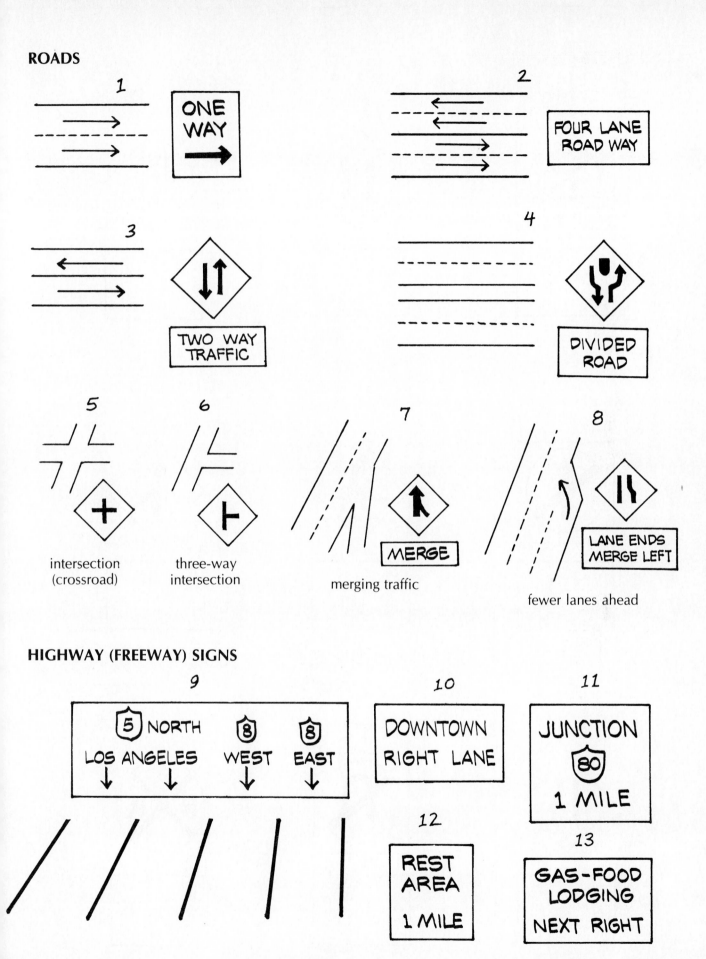

1

ONE WAY →

2

FOUR LANE ROAD WAY

3

TWO WAY TRAFFIC

4

DIVIDED ROAD

5
intersection (crossroad)

6
three-way intersection

7
MERGE

merging traffic

8
LANE ENDS MERGE LEFT

fewer lanes ahead

HIGHWAY (FREEWAY) SIGNS

9
⑤ NORTH ⑧ ⑧
LOS ANGELES WEST EAST

10
DOWNTOWN RIGHT LANE

11
JUNCTION 〈80〉 1 MILE

12
REST AREA 1 MILE

13
GAS-FOOD LODGING NEXT RIGHT

Write the information under the signs.

Read and discuss.

1. Drive on the right side of the road. Don't cross the center line.
2. Stay in your lane. Don't move around a lot.
3. Keep your eyes on the road.

4. Don't go too fast.
   Follow the speed limit signs.
   If the driving conditions are bad, you should go slower.

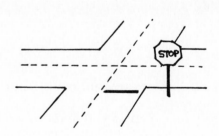

5. Don't go too slow in the fast lane (speed lane). Slow traffic should stay to the right side.
6. Don't follow too closely behind the car in front of you.
7. Be careful when you change lanes:
   a. Switch on the turn signal.
   b. Look in the rear view mirror.
   c. Turn and quickly look behind you.
   d. If the lane is clear, move over. Don't stop.
8. Stop at the line for a STOP sign or stop-light.
9. At a traffic signal, you must stop on the red light. If the light is yellow, stop if you can.
10. At a flashing yellow light, go slow and be careful.
    At a flashing red light, stop.

11. Right-of-way (who goes first?)
    a. The first car at a four-way STOP in-tersection should go first.
    b. If two cars arrive at an intersection at the same time, the car on the right should go first.

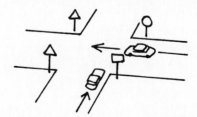

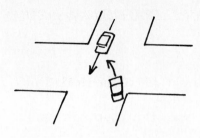

c. Left turn: let cars coming straight go by first, then turn left.

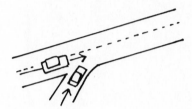

d. Merge: slow down and wait for the cars on the main road to go by, then move over. Don't stop!

12. Pedestrians (people walking) have the right-of-way.
    You should stop for them.

13. Move over for emergency vehicles.
    Go to the right side and stop.

14. Don't pass on a curve.
    Don't pass if you can't see in front of you.
    Don't pass on the right.

15. Car pool lanes are for cars with more than two people.
    Don't use them if you're driving alone.

16. Turn on your lights when it's dark or rainy or foggy.

17. Don't drive if you are very tired or angry or upset.
    Don't drive if you're drinking liquor.
    Don't drive if you're taking medicine that makes you sleepy.

18. Don't drive your car if it's in bad condition. If it has bad brakes, a broken headlight, bad tires, a noisy or leaky muffler—fix your car.

19. Don't drive without a license. Carry your driver's license with you when you drive. Keep a copy of your automobile registration paper in your car.

20. You should have automobile insurance. The insurance company will pay if you have an accident.

21. If you have an accident, don't hit and run. Stop and talk to the other driver. Write down the other person's name, telephone number, and driver's license number, and the name of his or her insurance company.

22. Don't hitchhike—it's very dangerous. Don't pick up somebody you don't know.

23. If you ride a motorcycle or bicycle, you have to follow the traffic laws.

24. Don't litter. Don't throw things out of your car onto the street.

SELF-TEST

A *Under the sign, write the number of the traffic law from pages 83–185.*

1.

2. NO PASSING ZONE

3. SLOW TRAFFIC KEEP RIGHT

___

___

___

4. TURN ON LIGHTS

5. ◇ LEFT LANE CAR POOLS 2 OR MORE ONLY

6. SLOW ROAD CONSTRUCTION NEXT 5 MILES

___

___

___

7. LEFT TURN YIELDS

8. STAY IN YOUR LANE

9. $ 100 FINE FOR LITTERING

___

___

___

B *Right or wrong?*

_____ 1. We can always drive as fast as the speed limit.

_____ 2. Drivers should stop for pedestrians.

_____ 3. If you're driving and you want to change lanes, stop and look behind you before you move over.

_____ 4. Every driver should have insurance.

_____ 5. When I drive my friend's car, I don't need a license.

_____ 6. If you drink, don't drive; if you drive, don't drink.

_____ 7. If you see an ambulance coming behind you, go faster.

_____ 8. Motorcycles can go on the freeway.

_____ 9. It's dangerous to follow another car too closely.

_____10. If you have an accident, drive away as fast as you can.

structure practice

A *Look at the examples and write.*

1. Driving is easy.
   It's easy to drive.

2. Riding a bicycle is not hard.
   It's not hard to ride a bicycle.

3. Traveling is fun.
   _____

4. Owning a car is expensive.
   _____

5. Driving is convenient.
   _____

6. Getting insurance is necessary.
   _____

7. Hitchhiking is very dangerous.
   _____

8. Walking alone at night isn't safe.
   _____

B *Look at the example and write.*

1. It's hard to save money.
   Saving money is hard.

2. It's very interesting to travel.
   _____

3. It's cheap to ride a bicycle.
   _____

4. It's not always convenient to take the bus.
   _____

5. It's important to know the traffic laws.
   _____

Orientation Notes: TICKETS

Read and discuss.

You can get a *ticket (citation)* if you break the traffic laws. You can get a *parking ticket* (parking violation)

1. if you park in the wrong place
2. if you don't put enough money in the parking meter
3. if you park in a place too long

The police will put a ticket on your car. You will have to pay a fine. Look at the ticket and see how much you have to pay. Then mail in the ticket with a check or money order.

Study these parking signs.

1. NO PARKING

2. NO PARKING 9 AM – 6 PM

3. NO PARKING TOW AWAY ZONE

4. ONE HOUR PARKING

5. 2 HOUR LIMIT

6. EMERGENCY PARKING ONLY

7. NO STOPPING 4 – 6 P.M.

8. PRIVATE PARKING VIOLATORS WILL BE TOWED

9. DO NOT BLOCK DRIVEWAY

10. HANDICAPPED ONLY

You can get a *driving ticket* (moving violation) for

1. speeding (driving too fast)
2. running a red light or a stop sign
3. going the wrong way on a one-way street
4. reckless driving (careless driving)
5. breaking other traffic laws

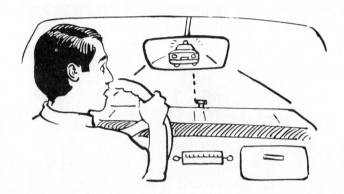

A police car will come up behind you. Pull over to the right and stop. The police officer will come and talk to you. The police officer may give you a *warning* (tell you to be more careful) or may give you a ticket. Look at the ticket carefully. You might have to pay a *fine*, or you might have to go to *court*.

If you go to court, you will talk to a *judge*. The judge will *decide* what to do about your case. In serious cases, or after many violations, your driver's license may be *suspended* (taken away for a short time) or *revoked* (taken away for at least one year). If you think the police officer was wrong, explain to the judge what happened; maybe the judge will let you go.

The Written Test

Read and discuss.

After you've studied the traffic laws in the Driver's Handbook, you're ready to take the written test. Look in the handbook for practice test questions and study them. Then go to the Motor Vehicle Department and take the written test.

Read the test questions and answers carefully. If you pass the test, you can get an instruction permit or go on to take the driving test. If you fail, you can study more and try again.

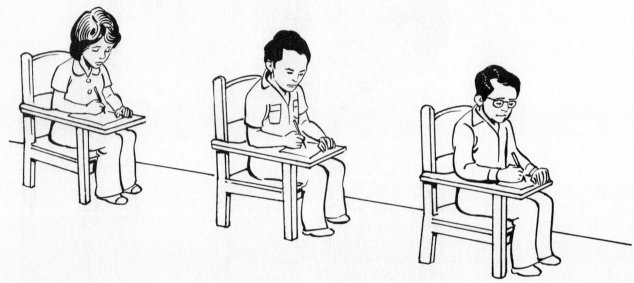

Mark an "X" in the box following the answer you think is correct.

Sample test questions

1. When you come to a stop sign, you should:
   a. slow down, and stop if necessary _____ ☐
   b. stop every time _____ ☐
   c. stop, unless nothing is coming _____ ☐
2. When two cars reach a corner from different streets at the same time, the legal right-of-way belongs to:
   a. the car on the right _____ ☐
   b. the car on the left _____ ☐
   c. the car moving faster _____ ☐
3. When an emergency vehicle comes up behind you, you should:
   a. stop where you are _____ ☐
   b. go faster _____ ☐
   c. pull over to the right and stop _____ ☐
4. Flashing red lights at a railroad crossing are a warning to:
   a. hurry _____ ☐
   b. slow down _____ ☐
   c. stop _____ ☐

The Driving Test

Read and discuss.

After you have passed the written test, you can take the driving test. Use your car or your friend's car. The *examiner* will sit next to you and tell you what to do. Usually you will drive around a practice area. The examiner will watch how you drive and will mark on a *score sheet*. At the end of the test the examiner will show you the paper and explain what you did wrong. If you make too many mistakes, you will fail the test, and you'll have to take it again.

■ *action sequence* ➡

     taking the test

For your driving test, the examiner will give you directions. He will tell you, for example:

1. Start the engine.
2. Pull out.
3. Go forward.
4. Stop at the stop sign.
5. Turn left.
6. Accelerate.
7. Change lanes.
8. Slow down.
9. Pull over to the curb.
10. Park.
11. Back up.
12. Stop.

Practice Driving Test

Look over the sample score sheet for a driving test. Then work with another student. You are the examiner, the other student is the **applicant.** *Give him or her the driving test. First fill out the top of the form. Then give the applicant directions, and mark the score sheet. At the end of the test, show the sheet to the applicant and explain what he or she did wrong. Then let the other student be the examiner.*

Name of Applicant				Place of Examination			Examiner		
Application Number				Date of Examination			Signature of Examiner		
	OK	poor	fail					OK	poor	fail
1. Starting				5. Attention						
a. seat belt				a. road signs and signals						
b. starting engine				b. correct speed						
c. caution				c. safe distance						
d. signals				d. concentration						
2. Control of vehicle				6. Right-of-way						
a. steering				a. stop sign						
b. shifting gears				b. yield						
c. accelerating				c. merge						
d. braking										
3. Turns				7. Parking						
a. signaling				a. signaling						
b. moving to and from correct lanes				b. braking						
c. too wide—too sharp				c. stopping						
				d. backing						
4. Lanes				e. parallel						
a. staying in lane										
b. changing lanes				TOTAL CHECKS			poor ____ ×1 = ____			
c. use of mirrors							fail ____ ×2 = ____			
d. looking behind					ADD FOR TOTAL SCORE _____					
e. passing				6 OR MORE = FAIL			PASS ☐ FAIL ☐			

structure practice

Study.

$$\left.\begin{array}{l} \text{I} \\ \text{you} \\ \text{she} \\ \text{etc.} \end{array}\right\} \quad \text{was/were} \underline{\hspace{2cm}} \text{ing}$$

Examples:

1. I was watching TV last night when I remembered I had to call my mother.

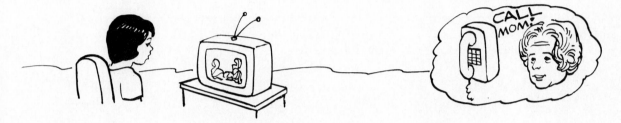

I was watching TV . . . when . . . I remembered!

2. As I was going to the kitchen, the telephone rang.

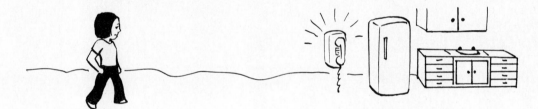

I was going to the kitchen . . . when . . . the phone rang!

3. It was my mother! She told me she was thinking about me and she decided to call. We were thinking about the same thing at the same time!

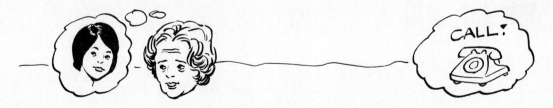

She was thinking about me . . . when . . . she decided to call!

Now look at the pictures and write a sentence.

1.

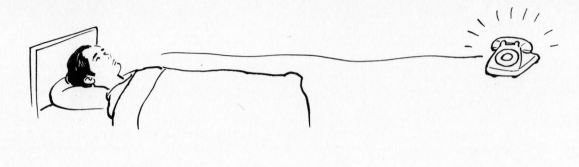

_____

2.

_____

3.

_____

Calling After an Accident

If you have a car accident, you should call your insurance company as soon as you can. Explain what happened and give them all the information.

A *Read and practice.*

Harry Phillips was driving to school at night and he had an accident. He called his insurance company in the morning.

Carol: Good morning. Bestco Insurance.

Harry: Hello. My name is Harry Phillips. I'm insured with you, and I had an accident last night.

Carol: What time?

Harry: About 6:45.

Carol: What happened?

Harry: I was driving down 16th Street on my way to school. It was raining. I stopped at the stop sign at B Street. I started to cross the street, but I didn't look carefully and I hit a car coming across in front of me.

Carol: So you were at fault?

Harry: Yes.

Carol: Was anyone hurt?

Harry: I think the other driver hurt her shoulder.

Carol: Did the police come?

Harry: Yes. They made a report.

Carol: What's the other driver's name?

Harry: Nancy Stevens. Her phone number is 231–6974.

Carol: All right. I'll call you back later. My name is Carol.

Harry: Thank you. Goodbye.

B *You had an accident! Look at the picture. Tell your insurance company what happened.*

What happened?

I was going _____ last night.
I was driving north on _____
and I came to _____ . The light
was _____ . _____
_____
_____

Who was at fault? _____

Was anyone injured? _____

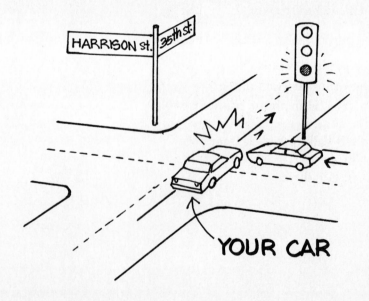

HARRISON st. 35th st.

YOUR CAR

Orientation Notes: *BUYING A CAR*

Read and discuss.

What kind of car should you buy?

First think about what you need and how much money you can spend. Don't buy a big car if you have a small family, and don't buy an expensive car if you don't have a lot of money.

Then think about the *expenses* of having a car:

1. gas
2. repairs (fixing your car)
3. insurance
4. registration

Small car or big car?

A small car is cheaper to run because it doesn't use a lot of gas. Big cars are strong and fast, but they use a lot of gas.

New car or used car?

A new car is very expensive. Usually you have to buy it on time payments. The insurance and registration for a new car are high.

A used car is cheaper, and maybe you can pay cash. The insurance and registration are cheaper, but maybe you will have to spend a lot of money to fix the car.

Where can you buy a car?

You can buy a car from a car company *(dealer)* or from another person. Look in the newspaper for AUTOMOBILES FOR SALE. The car dealer's prices are usually higher, but sometimes you can get a *guarantee* on the car.

What should the man think about before he decides to buy the car?

When you buy a car, get a good deal. Go around and look at a lot of cars. You don't have to pay the first price a salesman tells you. Ask him for a lower price. You can get a lower price for new cars too. You don't have to pay the price written on the car.

Be careful! People will tell you that their car is good, but maybe it's in bad condition. Look at the car, listen to the engine, look under the car, drive the car around *(test drive)*. Take a friend with you who knows about cars. Only buy a car if you're sure it's a good car at a good price.

listening and speaking

A *Listen to your teacher pronounce these words. Then listen again and repeat. Then listen to your teacher pronounce the key words below, and write under them the words that have the same sound in the same position. Check the word after you use it (√).*

save ( )   judge ( )   yellow ( )   sharp ( )
poor ( )   curve ( )   sure ( )
yes ( )   mark ( )( )   merge ( )( )

1	2	3	4	5	6
<u>y</u>ield	<u>m</u>otor	dri<u>v</u>e	chan<u>g</u>e	sta<u>rt</u>	y<u>our</u>

_____   _____   _____   _____   _____   _____

_____   _____   _____   _____   _____   _____

Now think, and write one more word for each number.

_____   _____   _____   _____   _____

B *Circle the cluster and pronounce.*

stop   stick   straight   street   slow

sleep   speed   score   switch   practice

private   flash   trunk   try   travel

traffic   drink   drive

feel
fill
fail
fell
fall
full

PRACTICE THESE WORDS

C *Your teacher will pronounce these words. Listen and repeat.*

de part ment   man u al   au to ma tic   ex a mi ner

ne ces sa ry   ex a mi na tion

Now pronounce these words and write them above in the correct column.

accident   motorcycle   pedestrian   important   signature
violation   carefully   temporary   transmission

Community Services

chapter five

COMPETENCIES:
1. Use postal services: buy stamps, send letters and packages
2. Fill out postal forms
3. Handle mail appropriately
4. Recognize signs found in recreational areas
5. Recognize illegal activities and report to police
6. Take precautions for self-protection

ORIENTATION:
1. Post office services
2. Dealing with mail
3. Schools
4. Recreation
5. Laws, breaking the law, and law enforcement (including court system)
6. Self-protection and crime prevention
7. Structure and responsibilities of government

STRUCTURES:
1. Conditional with *would, if*-clause

Teacher Notes and Suggestions

Page 102   1. Introduce the topic of the post office by asking students if they write letters; if they send letters inside the United States or to foreign countries; how much it costs to send letters; where they buy stamps; and similar questions.
2. Adjust the dialogue if necessary for current postal rates.
3. Review the comparative form of adjectives, found in *Sending a letter*.
4. Registered letters can be sent inside and outside of the United States.
5. If possible, show students real post office forms.

Page 103   1. Your students may often send letters and packages to foreign countries and might need to know about procedures such as registered letters and customs declarations. Ask the students in the class who have sent packages to explain how they did it and what was involved.
2. You may want to point out in the dialogue the use of *would* for possibility. The use of *take* in time expressions should also be pointed out.

Page 104   1. Introduce the topic by asking the students if they get letters (mail) at their house. Ask what they would do if they got a letter addressed to a name they don't know; draw an example letter on the blackboard and demonstrate the procedure, as is shown on the top of the page. Then give another situation, where students might receive mail for a relative or friend who has moved away from the house. Draw another example letter and show what to do, as explained in the second paragraph of the page. Then read the first two paragraphs in class.
2. In studying about change of address cards, have real or practice forms for students to fill out. Give them a "new address" to put on the form.
3. Students might not be able to recognize what mail is important and what is not; bring in examples of junk mail to show the class.

Page 106   Introduce the topic by talking about the school and school system you are in. Relate it to the overall education system in your community. Ask if anyone in the class has attended American high school or has children now attending school. Explain the schooling process in your own words; then read and discuss the page as suggested on page *viii*. Use the questions for further discussion.

Pages 107 to 108   Introduce the topic by asking what students like to do in their free time, what they do for fun. Ask if they ever go to parks, play sports, go fishing, and so on. Then read and discuss, using the questions for further discussion.

Page 109   Explain what the signs mean and where they might be found. After students have listed the signs from below, set the signs in a situational context and ask the students how they would react to them.

Page 110   Introduce by asking if any students like to fish and if any have gone fishing in the United States. Procedures here may be very new to them. Explain as is done at the top of the page, then present the given situation and practice; role-play this and the following page.

Page 111   This situation is an example of law enforcement and judicial processes and shows the seriousness with which Americans take laws and regulations. After practicing the dialogue, discuss the situation, comparing it with what would happen in the students' native countries.

Page 112   Introduce the topic by asking if any students have had contact with police in this country, and under what circumstances. Ask if anyone has been a victim of some crime; discuss. Read and discuss, using the questions for further discussion.

Page 113   Ask the students what they think about American police. Ask if any students have ever called or talked to the police. Explain the role of laws, police, and public citizens in the society. Read and discuss the top of the page. Then explain that people can help stop crimes by taking care of themselves as suggested in the list of "good ideas for your safety."

Page 114   1. Structure: *if*-clause with *would*.

2. Before referring to the page, give a few examples of problems, perhaps suggested by the preceding pages about crimes, and ask what students' reactions would be. Class then answers the questions on the page and discusses the reactions given.

The Post Office

U.S.

Read and practice.

Buying stamps

You can buy stamps at the post office.

Man:	I want some stamps.
Clerk:	What kind?
Man:	Ten 20's and five 40's.
Clerk:	What else?
Man:	Four aerogrammes.
Clerk:	Is that all?
Man:	Yes, that's all.
Clerk:	OK, that's $5.20.

foreign airmail

aerogramme

Sending a letter

Put the correct *postage* on your letter and put it in a mailbox. Write your address on the letter (return address). If you're sending a heavy letter, you may need more stamps. The clerk will tell you how much it will cost.

If you're sending a letter *overseas* (to a *foreign* country), you can send it *air mail* (by airplane) or *surface mail* (by land or sea). Air mail is faster, but it's more expensive. Surface mail is cheaper, but it's slower.

Sending a registered letter

If you want to mail an important letter or a check, you can send it *registered*. You have to fill out a form. It's expensive to send a registered letter, but sometimes it's a good idea.

I want to send this letter registered.

The charge is $3.50.

	Reg. Fee $ 3.50	AUG. 14 1984
	Postage $ .40	
FROM	ELLEN HOW	
	615 SIMPSON ST.	
	SAN FRANCISCO, CA	ZIP CODE 94108
	IRENE CHAN	
TO	72 BEACH DR. Apt. 12	
	HONOLULU, HA.	ZIP CODE 96841

Sending a Package

Read and practice.

The postage for sending a package depends on the size and weight. You can send a package *first class* (air mail), but it's very expensive. *Parcel post* is surface mail, and it's much cheaper.

Woman: I want to send this package to New York.

Clerk: First class or parcel post?

Woman: How much would it be each way?

Clerk: First class would be $8.65, parcel post $1.72.

Woman: How long would it take parcel post?

Clerk: About two weeks.

Woman: That's all right. Send it parcel post.

If you send a package to a foreign country, you have to fill out a form *(customs declaration)*.

Look at the form and answer the questions below.

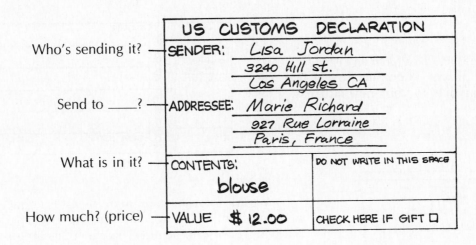

1. Who is sending the package? _____
2. Who is she sending it to? _____
3. Where is the package going? _____
4. What is she sending? _____
5. What is the value? _____

Read and discuss.

The mailman from the post office *delivers* mail to everyone's house. If you get mail that is not for you, give it back to the mailman. If it is for someone who moved away, you can write "Moved" on the front of the envelope.

If you get mail for a relative or friend who was living with you but moved away, you can send it to him or her by writing "Please forward" and the new address on the envelope. Then give it back to the mailman or mail it again.

If you move, fill out a *change of address* card at the post office. Then the post office will forward your mail to your new address.

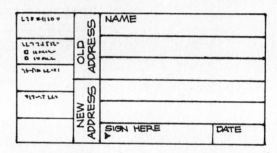

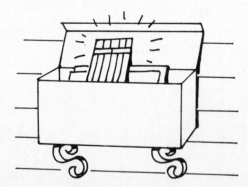

A pink form in your mailbox shows that someone sent you a special letter or package but you weren't home to receive it. You can go to the post office to pick it up.

Everybody gets letters from businesses they don't know. Sometimes we call this *junk mail.* The businesses want to sell you something. If you see that mail is not important, you can throw it away.

Filling Out Postal Forms

Fill out the forms.

1. You're sending a shirt to your friend back in your country. The value of the shirt is $9.00.

2. You're sending a check to your parents and you want to register the letter. The registration fee is $3.50 and the postage is $.80.

3. You're moving on the first day of next month and you want to let the post office know. Your new address is 435 Delta Dr., Sacramento, CA 95814. Your whole family is moving.

4. Your brother moved away from your house last week. His new address is 5321 Buckley Road, Denver, Colorado. Forward this letter to him.

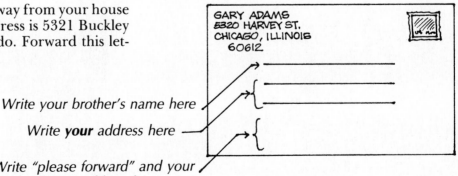

Write your brother's name here

*Write **your** address here*

Write "please forward" and your brother's new address here

Orientation Notes: SCHOOLS

Read and discuss.

Education is available for all people in America. We begin as young children and can continue as adults. There are *public* schools (run by the government) and *private* schools (often run by churches). Public schools are usually free (except universities). You have to *register* your children for school when you move into a new neighborhood.

Children begin school at age 4 or 5, and they must attend school until the age of 16. In public schools boys and girls study together. Students are in class six or seven hours a day. They study English, mathematics, social studies (history, geography, and government), science, art, music, and physical education. In high school students can also study languages, business, machine shop, and other courses. Later some students go to the university to study to become teachers, engineers, business managers, lawyers, doctors, and so on. These schools have many *activities* for students: sports, *clubs,* movies, shows, and dances. There are also adult schools or community colleges for people who want to continue their education in their free time.

Schools usually have counselors to help students plan their studies and their future and to help them with problems. Many schools now have problems with smoking, drugs, sex, or with students' bad *behavior* or bad *attitude.* Parents can go to the school any time to talk to the counselors about their children's problems. Many parents join *groups,* sometimes called PTA—Parent and Teacher Association. All parents should go to school *meetings,* visit the schools, and talk to teachers to find out what their children are doing in school.

Answer these questions and discuss them in class.

1. Do you have children in school now? What grade are they in?
2. Did you ever go to visit their school?
3. Did you ever talk to the teachers?
4. What do your children tell you about their school?
5. Can everyone go to school in your country?
6. Is it easy to get into high school or university there?
7. Is education free in your country?
8. Are there any problems in the schools there?

Orientation Notes: RECREATION

Read and discuss.

      Everybody likes to have fun, Americans too. Americans often have a lot of free time and on weekends and vacations they like to go places. Most American cities have parks, where people can go to have a *picnic,* play sports, walk around, or just sit and relax.

      Most states have forests or mountains, where people like to go *hiking, camping, skiing,* or *hunting.* Fishing is also very *popular.* Usually you need a license for fishing or hunting, and you have to follow the laws.

      When the weather is hot, people like to enjoy the sun and go swimming at pools or beaches.

SPORTS

Americans like sports very much. Baseball, football, basketball, golf, tennis, and soccer are very popular. Many people like to play sports, other people like to watch. Every weekend there are many sports programs on television.

AT NIGHT

A lot of Americans like to go out at night, especially on weekends. They go to restaurants, movie theaters, bars, and places where they can dance or listen to music.

Answer these questions and discuss them in class.

1. Are there parks near your house? Where?
2. What do you like to do in your free time?
3. What kinds of activities are popular in your country?
4. What are your favorite sports?
5. Do you like to play or watch?
6. Do you like to go out at night? What do you like to do?

Signs

Read and discuss.

In recreation areas you often see signs. Signs can tell you:

1. You shouldn't do something.

2. You shouldn't go in.

3. Danger.

4. Take care of the park.

5. Be clean.

Now add one more sign from below to each group.

Fishing

Read and discuss.

If you want to go fishing in the United States, you usually need a license. You can get one at a government office, at fishing shops, and sometimes at lakes. At some lakes you have to pay a fee to go fishing. There is sometimes a limit to the number and size of fish you can catch. If you don't follow the rules, you might have to pay a fine.

Read and practice.

Dan went fishing at Bear Lake. He didn't have a license. He was out all day and caught 22 fish. He didn't know the limit was only 15. When he was leaving, a *ranger* (park policeman) came and talked to him.

Ranger: Hello there. I see you're doing very well.

Dan: Hi. Yes. They're really biting today.

Ranger: Can I see your license?

Dan: Sorry, I don't have one.

Ranger: You don't? You gotta (you have to) have one, you know.

Dan: I know, but I didn't get one yet.

Ranger: Do you know there's a limit of 15 fish? How many have you got?

Dan: Oh, I didn't know! I have 22.

Ranger: I'm going to have to give you a citation. You'll have to go to court and talk to a judge.

Dan: But I didn't know. You can keep the fish.

Ranger: Too late now. You'll get a notice in the mail.

At Court

Read and practice.

Dan got a notice to *appear* in court. He had to go to the County Courthouse and report to Courtroom 6.

Clerk:	Dan Lee!
Judge:	You are charged with violations of the fish and game laws: fishing without a license and exceeding the limit. How do you plead?
Dan:	Guilty.*
Judge:	Do you have anything to say?
Dan:	I didn't know about the limit. I was fishing to get food for my family.
Judge:	How long have you been in the United States?
Dan:	About six months.
Judge:	How long have you been fishing here?
Dan:	Maybe three months.
Judge:	Don't you know you need a license?
Dan:	I know, but I didn't get one yet because I didn't have the money.
Judge:	Well, there are laws we all have to follow here. You will have a fine of $30 for fishing without a license, and a fine of $1.00 per fish over the limit. Can you pay that?
Dan:	Yes.
Judge:	And if you're going to continue fishing, you'll have to get a license.
Dan:	Yes, I will.
Judge:	All right. You may go.

*guilty = I did something wrong
innocent = I didn't do anything wrong

Orientation Notes: *BREAKING THE LAW*

Read and discuss.

We have laws that people must follow. If you break the law (make a violation), the police can stop you. For a driving violation, such as speeding or driving without a license, you might have to pay a fine or go to traffic court.

For serious violations *(crimes)*, the police can *arrest* you and take you to the police station. Usually you can call your family or talk to a *lawyer.* Sometimes the police might put you in *jail,* and your family or friends might have to pay some money *(bail)* before you can go home. Later you will probably have to go to court.

If someone does something to you, you can take that person to court. If it's serious, you need to get a lawyer to help you. Lawyers are very expensive, but some cities have Legal Aid Service to help poor people find lawyers. Court cases usually take a long time—sometimes over a year. If the problem is not too serious, you can go to Small Claims Court. It's fast and you don't need a lawyer.

If you see a crime or if something happens to you, call the police. Maybe they can catch the *criminal* (law breaker). They will also send more police cars to go around your neighborhood.

These are some serious crimes:

1. Stealing (robbery)
2. Stealing something from a store by not paying (shoplifting)
3. Breaking something (vandalism)
4. Attacking someone (assault)
5. Carrying a weapon
6. Rape
7. Killing (murder)
8. Hitting your wife (wife beating)
9. Hitting or hurting your children (child abuse)
10. Using or having street drugs, such as marijuana
11. Drunk driving
12. Making fires (arson)

Discuss.

1. Are these crimes in your country?
2. Is there a lot of crime in your neighborhood here?
3. Have you or has anyone you know ever been robbed or attacked?
4. Have you ever gone to court?

Orientation Notes: POLICE

Read and discuss.

City and state governments have police to *protect* people and to *enforce* the laws. Their job is often hard and dangerous. Police ride around the city in cars and look for problems. They also watch for traffic violations.

When you call the police about some problem, they send someone out to talk to you. The *police officer* (policeman) asks questions, gets the information, and makes a *report*.

Hello, I'm Officer Barrett. You called about a problem?

Yes, somebody broke my window. Please come in.

GOOD IDEAS FOR YOUR SAFETY

Read and discuss.

Most people in America are nice, but there are some bad people. They might rob you or hurt you. Here are some things you can do to protect yourself.

1. Always keep your doors locked. When you go out, lock the doors and windows. Turn on a light if you're going to be out at night. If you're going away for a few days, ask your friends or neighbors to watch your house.
2. When you leave your car, lock it and take your keys.
3. Don't go walking around in a bad area.
4. Don't go out alone at night.
5. Watch your children. Tell them not to talk to *strangers* (people you don't know).
6. Don't take a ride from a stranger. Don't hitchhike.

What Would You Do?

Study. Fill in the blanks and discuss. Then practice with another student.

1. If you saw an accident, what would you do?

   I would call the police.

2. If somebody bothered you or hit you, what would you do?

   _____

3. If you saw somebody break your window or damage your car, what would you do?

   _____

4. If you were out walking and somebody stole your purse or your wallet, what would you do?

   _____

5. If somebody with a weapon tried to rob you, what would you do?

   _____

6. If somebody stopped you on the street and asked you for money, what would you do?

   _____

7. If you went home and saw somebody in your house, what would you do?

   _____

8. If you were sleeping and heard somebody in your house, what would you do?

   _____

Orientation Notes: GOVERNMENT

Read and discuss.

There are four *levels* of government in the United States.

1. *Federal government* (national government, U.S. government). The federal government is in Washington, D.C., the *capital* of the United States. The *President* is the top government *official*. The *Congress* of *senators* and *representatives* makes laws for our country. The federal government takes care of the *Armed Services*, the Post Office, Social Security, *immigration, passports,* and *customs.* Everybody pays taxes to pay for the government.

2. *State government.* Every state has a government, in the state capital. The top official of the state is the *governor.* The state congress (state legislature) makes laws for the state. The state government takes care of highways, employment, licenses (driving, teaching, doctors), and forests. We pay tax to the state government, too, including sales tax and gasoline tax.

3. *County government.* States have many counties, and counties have governments. They usually don't make laws, but they help the state government with taxes, health departments, education, courts, and social services. They keep *records* of births, deaths, and marriages.

4. *City government.* Cities also have governments. The top official is usually called a *mayor.* The *city council* makes laws for the city. Cities take care of schools, police, fire department, transportation (buses, trains, airports), parks, business licenses, building permits, streets, and garbage collection. Some cities charge taxes too.

Voting

We elect government *officials* by voting in *elections.* We have new elections every few years, and if our officials are not good, we can vote for new people. In America only *citizens* can vote.

Write the names of

1. the President of the United States   _____

2. the governor of your state   _____

3. the mayor of your city   _____

listening and speaking

A *Listen to your teacher pronounce these words. Then listen again and repeat. Then listen to your teacher pronounce the key words below, and write under them the words that have the same sound in the same position. Check the word after you use it.*

club ( )
would ( )
rob ( ) ( )

birth ( )
vote ( )
death ( )

very ( ) ( )
wrong ( )
put ( )

air ( )

1	2	3	4	5	6
<u>v</u>alue	<u>r</u>ule	jo<u>b</u>	wi<u>th</u>	l<u>oo</u>k	th<u>ere</u>
_____	_____	_____	_____	_____	_____
_____	_____	_____	_____	_____	_____

Now think, and write one more word for each number.

_____ _____ _____ _____ _____ _____

B *Read these names for practice.*

<table>
<tr><td colspan="3">men</td><td colspan="2">women</td></tr>
<tr><td>John</td><td>Mike</td><td>Ken</td><td>Jan</td><td>Laurie</td></tr>
<tr><td>Jim</td><td>Mark</td><td>Kevin</td><td>Jane</td><td>Mary</td></tr>
<tr><td>Joe</td><td>Rick</td><td>Chris</td><td>Jean</td><td>Nancy</td></tr>
<tr><td>Jack</td><td>Ron</td><td>Greg</td><td>Joan</td><td>Sue</td></tr>
<tr><td>Jerry</td><td>Don</td><td>Gary</td><td>Joanne</td><td>Cathy</td></tr>
<tr><td>Bill</td><td>Dan</td><td>Charlie</td><td>Ann</td><td>Carol</td></tr>
<tr><td>Bob</td><td>Dave</td><td>Steve</td><td>Diane</td><td>Karen</td></tr>
<tr><td>Pete</td><td>Dennis</td><td>Larry</td><td>Fran</td><td>Chris</td></tr>
<tr><td>Pat</td><td>Tim</td><td>Lou</td><td>Ellen</td><td>Gail</td></tr>
<tr><td>Fred</td><td>Tom</td><td>Al</td><td>Helen</td><td>Pat</td></tr>
<tr><td>Frank</td><td>Ted</td><td>Ed</td><td>Linda</td><td>Pam</td></tr>
</table>

C *Your teacher will pronounce these words. Listen and repeat.*

_ ´
po lice
re port
ap pear

_ ´ _
de li ver
e lec tion

´ _ _
go vern ment
re gis ter
ci ti zen
na tio nal

_ _ ´ _
trans por ta tion

_ ´ _ _
ge o gra phy

_ _ ´ _ _
re pre sen ta tive

_ _ _ ´ _
as so ci a tion

Now pronounce these words and write them above in the correct column.

president   history   arrest   official   capital   immigration

protect   popular   neighborhood

116   Chapter Five

Appendix

irregular verbs

Base Form	Past	Past Participle	Base Form	Past	Past Participle
be	was	been	know	knew	known
break	broke	broken	leave	left	left
bring	brought	brought	lose	lost	lost
buy	bought	bought	make	made	made
catch	caught	caught	meet	met	met
come	came	come	put	put	put
cost	cost	cost	read	read	read
cut	cut	cut	ride	rode	ridden
do	did	done	ring	rang	rung
drink	drank	drunk	run	ran	run
drive	drove	driven	say	said	said
eat	ate	eaten	see	saw	seen
fall	fell	fallen	sell	sold	sold
feel	felt	felt	send	sent	sent
fight	fought	fought	sing	sang	sung
find	found	found	sit	sat	sat
fit	fit	fit	sleep	slept	slept
fly	flew	flown	speak	spoke	spoken
forget	forgot	forgotten	spend	spent	spent
freeze	froze	frozen	steal	stole	stolen
get	got	gotten	take	took	taken
give	gave	given	teach	taught	taught
go	went	gone	tell	told	told
have	had	had	think	thought	thought
hear	heard	heard	understand	understood	understood
hit	hit	hit	wake	woke	woken
hurt	hurt	hurt	win	won	won
keep	kept	kept	write	wrote	written